The Evolution of Bitcoin: A Beginner's Absolute Guide to Bitcoin and Blockchains

A Step-by-Step Guide to Building Long-Term Wealth With Bitcoin, Blockchain, and Cryptocurrency Investments in 2021 and Beyond

Matthew Law

Table of Contents

Introduction

Since its creation little over a decade ago, Bitcoin has seen epic rises and equally epic falls. Once an outlier in the financial markets, Bitcoin and other cryptocurrencies, known as altcoins, are slowly being accepted by businesses, governments, and financial institutions around the world. However, we are nowhere near to seeing the heights that Bitcoin and altcoins have to offer, and opportunity is still rife on many fronts.

Along with Bitcoin is the blockchain—a potentially revolutionary technology that not only provides a new way to store and track data but has the potential to change the way we keep and track data in the supply chain and beyond.

With more prominent people and businesses investing in Bitcoin, it's clear that Bitcoin is not going to fall to the wayside anytime soon. Likewise, with the number of tools and apps out there, anyone can invest in Bitcoin and other cryptocurrencies with as little as $10. However, is it worth investing in this growing fad? The answer to that is yes, it can be, but as you will see, investing in crypto is not for the faint of heart.

What This Book Has to Offer

The goal of this book is to provide you with the best, most complete introduction to Bitcoin and the blockchain technology that runs it, as well as how to get started in investing in Bitcoin and other altcoins.

By the time you have reached the end of this book, you will be armed with the information necessary to not only understand what Bitcoin and altcoins are but also to begin investing in cryptocurrency. We will also go through some simple investing strategies to get you started and show you ways how to safeguard your investment.

To this end, we will introduce you to Bitcoin, including how it works, some of its history, and delve a bit into why it is both so popular and divisive. We will also be looking at the inner workings of the blockchain, explaining how it works, and why it is not only key for making cryptocurrency what it is but also touch on some of its other untapped potential. We will also talk about crypto mining, its importance to blockchain technology, and how it can potentially make a profit.

With this basic understanding, we will then look at the different tools needed to invest in Bitcoin and other altcoins—mainly, crypto wallets and the crypto exchanges where one goes to buy and sell. We will also talk about a few of the most common altcoins and their potential alongside Bitcoin.

Finally, we end with some strategies on how to manage your crypto investment, including ways of making profit without selling any of your coins or even buying any in the first place. We will also talk a bit about the potential future of Bitcoin and cryptocurrency in general.

Overall, we hope that you will find this book interesting and informative; this book will be able to help you get started in investing in cryptocurrency.

About the Author

Matthew Law has been trading Bitcoin for over 12 years and is an expert in the cryptocurrency field. They write articles to help people make a living off Bitcoin and various cryptocurrencies—making it a point to stay on top of the crypto business. Through years of education and coaching, Law specializes in helping people realize their full potential in the cryptocurrency market and beyond.

Chapter 1:

Bitcoin and Cryptocurrency

Basics

When Bitcoin was first introduced in 2009 by Satoshi Nakamoto, it was envisioned as a new, decentralized digital currency that could operate without the interference of banks and governments. Satoshi himself saw Bitcoin as a digital asset—one that could be used as a currency for online transactions. Even today, Bitcoin still lives up to this vision. No one group or entity controls the Bitcoin network, and no particular government has any control over Bitcoin, though many are trying to regulate the cryptocurrency industry.

Part Cash, Part Asset

To fully understand Bitcoin, one has to first understand that Bitcoin and all other cryptocurrencies are considered both a currency and an asset.

No one argues Bitcoin's status as a currency. Only 21 million bitcoins will ever be mined. Thanks to the blockchain, bitcoin transactions are easy to track and are validated by miners before they are added to the blockchain itself, where they effectively become set in stone. While it is getting easier for one to buy Bitcoin, only a small percentage of people actually have bitcoins and other altcoins in their possession.

This should eventually change now that more and more businesses are accepting Bitcoin and other cryptos as payment. Microsoft, Home Depot, and Starbucks are a few of the businesses that accept Bitcoin, while online stores like Newegg or Overstock and even the streaming platform Twitch accept Bitcoin and some other altcoins as payment. PayPal, one of the largest online payment processors in the world, now allows you to not only buy, sell, and hold Bitcoin and a few other altcoins but also to use those coins when making purchases through their platform.

However, because of its rising price and popularity, Bitcoin is also being seen as a safe-haven asset akin to gold. As the markets go down, particularly during the COVID-19 pandemic, Bitcoin's price continues to rise, allowing for a positive return on investment. However, unlike gold's more stable price, Bitcoin's volatility makes it a riskier investment—a risk that more and more investors are keen on taking.

Being able to both hold on to Bitcoin for investment, or to spend it, makes Bitcoin a versatile currency. However, in the current market, bitcoin is trending more toward an investment type asset than a currency to be spent. Altcoins, another name for other cryptos that are not Bitcoin—like Litecoin and Ethereum—might fill the role of being a more spending-type crypto in the future. However, for now, Bitcoin is still king and will likely continue to be king for some time.

The Birth of Bitcoin

Though there have been various efforts to create a viable digital currency in the past, most of them were either short lived or never got out of the starting gate. The earliest attempt at digital currency that was implemented was DigiCash, founded in 1989 by David Chaum. Unfortunately, DigiCash was only accepted by two banks in the United States before it was forced to declare bankruptcy in 1998.

Though DigiCash would not prove successful, it would open the doors for others to try developing a digital currency of their own. The most successful of these would be Hashcash, a proof-of-work type of system. Hashcash was not just a type of digital currency, but the system also had other uses, including cutting down on email spam. There were also several attempts at creating a digital currency that never got out of the starting gate, such as Wei Dai's "B-Money" and Nick Szabo's "Bit Gold." Both would fail to secure start-up funds, but their white papers would eventually help influence the creation of Bitcoin.

Perhaps the most successful attempt at creating a digital currency prior to Bitcoin would be PayPal. Though not an actual digital currency, PayPal revolutionized the way online payments were done by providing a secure way to transfer money through a web browser. Even today, PayPal is easily one of the largest online payment processors in the world.

Bitcoin itself was first introduced to the world on October 31, 2008, when a white paper authored by Satoshi Nakamoto titled, *Bitcoin: A Peer-to-Peer Electronic Cash System*, was uploaded to a crypto mailing list.

Based on some of the concepts from previous attempts at creating a digital currency, Satoshi outlined a decentralized digital currency using the blockchain to record transactions. Its decentralized nature would ensure that no one person or power would have control over the currency, while the blockchain would make the currency almost completely hack-proof.

Bitcoin's genesis block, the first block in Bitcoin's blockchain, would be mined shortly after on January 3rd, 2009. The first Bitcoin transaction would occur nine days later on January 12th, 2009, when Hal Finney received 10 bitcoins from Satoshi after downloading the Bitcoin software. The first commercial transaction would occur the next year on 17 May 2010, when Laszlo Haneycz purchased two pizzas for 10,000 bitcoins (Wikipedia Foundation, 2021c).

Satoshi would continue work on the Bitcoin software in collaboration with other programmers until mid-2010, when he gave control of the source code and the network alert keys to Gavin Anderson before completely disappearing. Not long after, people soon realized that Satoshi Nakamoto was a pseudonym, and to this day, Satoshi's identity remains a mystery.

Satoshi Nakamoto: Who Was He?

According to his 2012 P2P Foundation profile, Satoshi Nakamoto was a 37-year-old male living in Japan. However, in his various correspondence, as well as in the Bitcoin source code itself, Satoshi used language and terms associated with British English. There was also this piece of text embedded in Bitcoin's genesis block: "The Times 03/Jan/2009 Chancellor on brink of second bailout for banks" (Wikipedia Foundation, 2021e).

This note served as both a time stamp and commentary on the traditional banking system. However, the note itself refers specifically to a newspaper that publishes in the United Kingdom. This, along with the use of British English, has led some to theorize that Satoshi may have been from the United Kingdom or one of the commonwealth nations.

While some think Satoshi may be an eccentric genius, others believe that rather than a single person, Satoshi Nakamoto may have in fact been a group of people working together to develop Bitcoin. Given the size and scope of the development of the blockchain and the Bitcoin software, it is quite feasible for the software to have been built by a group of people rather than a single person. Whether Satoshi was indeed a single person or a group of people with one potentially British man serving as the spokesperson of the group, we may never know.

Despite the time that has gone by, no one has come close to identifying who Satoshi Nakamoto really is. There have been a number of guesses and investigations, with many people named as potentially being Nakamoto. Even Elon Musk was suggested as being Nakamoto, though this has since been debunked.

Why Satoshi hid his identity is an equally interesting mystery. As the man who created Bitcoin and the first to implement the blockchain, Nakamoto would be quite famous. Perhaps he wished to keep his privacy, or, for whatever reason, he did not wish to be associated with his creation.

During his time, Satoshi also mined countless bitcoin blocks himself. In 2009, for example, 32,489 blocks were mined. At a block reward of 50 bitcoins per block, this comes to a total sum of 1,624,450 bitcoins mined that year (Frankenfield, 2021g). As potentially one of the few miners in 2009, it's quite possible Satoshi received the lion's share of these coins.

No one is certain how many coins Nakamoto currently has, but by the current value of Bitcoin, he may be a very wealthy man. This would make him a prime target for thieves and hackers, so his anonymity would go a long way in keeping his coins safe.

This, however, assumes Nakamoto kept the coins he collected prior to his disappearance. It's also possible that Nakamoto is still very active in the Bitcoin trade under a different pseudonym. Of course, it's also possible he died shortly after handing the source code and keys to Gavin Andersen, who would go on to become the lead developer of the Bitcoin software until 2014. This would ensure his legacy would live on if he knew his time on this Earth would soon be over.

Sadly, the mystery of Satoshi Nakamoto is one that may never be answered. But regardless of who Satoshi is, no one can deny his contribution as the creator of cryptocurrency.

Bitcoin's Link to Crime

Once Bitcoin made its way out of the trial stages and proved to be a legitimate digital currency, it wouldn't be long before criminals saw the potential of crypto. Bitcoin would be used in place of cash, and various black markets would also adopt Bitcoin as their primary payment method. The first and perhaps most well-known of these was the Silk Road.

Founded in February of 2011, the Silk Road was the first online darknet market. It primarily sold drugs but also fake drivers licenses. Silk Road did not allow the sale anything that could harm or defraud others, including child pornography, weapons, stolen credit cards, or assassination contracts (Wikipedia Foundation, 2021x).

All of the Silk Road's sales were done in Bitcoin through a system where coins would be held in escrow until the product was delivered to the buyer. The site also employed a hedging mechanism where sellers could opt to fix the price of the bitcoins at time of sale in USD to mitigate Bitcoin's volatility. The site's founder, Ross Ulbritcht, also known as the Dread Pirate Roberts, would also cover any changes in the price of bitcoins during an item's transit (Wikipedia, 2021x).

The Silk Road came to an end in October of 2013, when Ross Ulbritcht was arrested by the FBI. At the time, the FBI Initially seized 26,000 bitcoins and would later seize an additional 144,000 bitcoins, each worth at the time up to $28.5 million respectively (Wikipedia, 2021x). At today's prices, those same coins would be worth roughly $8 billion.

Though the Silk Road was shut down, Bitcoin—and later on, other altcoins—would still be used by criminals to move money around. The Silk Road also started the notion that Bitcoin was only good for criminals and not as a legitimate currency. This stigma would be banished for the most part as time moved on.

Currently, only a small percentage of crypto transactions are related to crime. Better technologies and oversight by law enforcement organizations around the world, coupled with more regulation of cryptocurrency, has led to Bitcoin and other altcoins being used less for criminal activity. However, Bitcoin and other altcoins are still a preferred method of payment for some cyber criminals, including as payment in ransomware attacks.

Why Is Bitcoin So Popular?

While one can probably find any number of reasons why Bitcoin and other altcoins are rising in popularity, there have always been two fundamental reasons why Bitcoin and crypto have captured the fascination of many.

Bitcoin Is Decentralized

Bitcoin's original appeal was its decentralized nature. Though we will go into more detail a little later, Bitcoin works on a decentralized platform. Anyone can join Bitcoin's network by running the Bitcoin software and adding their computing power to the network. However, the network itself is considered trustless: All nodes on the network are equal, and no single node has authority over another. In order to make changes to the network, you must have the consensus of all or at least an overwhelming majority. If not everyone in the network is in agreement with the change, a hard fork can occur. (We will explain this in more detail in the next chapter.)

This decentralized nature of the network means that no one person or entity can control it. This also means that no one government or financial institution can control Bitcoin. In order to do so, they would need to control a majority of the node network. This appeals to many who are critics of traditional money policy and the meddling that goes on within it.

Bitcoin's decentralized nature also means that it has no one point of failure. Even if a few nodes in the network go down, the rest of the network will continue on working. This makes it very difficult for Bitcoin or any other altcoin to be hacked.

Even if you were to hack one node on the network, its errant code and data would be rejected by the rest of the network.

Bitcoin Is Secure

As we will go into more detail in the next chapter, Bitcoin and any cryptocurrency running on the blockchain is almost impossible to hack. Aside from the decentralized network, the blockchain itself is a very tamper-resistant entity. Once a transaction has been added to the blockchain, it may as well be set in stone. Moreover, there is not just one copy of the blockchain on the network: Each node will have either a full or partial copy of the completed blockchain.

As previously mentioned, the only way to change anything on the network is to have control over a majority of it. Such a feat, known as the 51% attack, would require monumental resources to pull for a network the size of Bitcoin. At the time of writing, there are 12,835 active nodes in the Bitcoin network (Avan-Nomayo, 2021). For someone to take over the network, they would need to control a minimum of 6,174 of those nodes.

This is all technically true, but as you might guess from the various stories of Bitcoin thefts and hacks over the years, the system is not perfect. While Bitcoin and the blockchain are incredibly secure, the systems that hold and move the currency around are not always as secure. These systems are points of weakness in the cryptocurrency network that hackers can and have successfully exploited. We will discuss this topic in more detail later on, but for now, remember that crypto itself is almost completely hack-proof.

Chapter 2:

The Blockchain

It is not very often that a new technology comes along that has the true capacity to revolutionize and fundamentally change how we do a particular task. The blockchain is such a technology. The way blockchain manages and stores data transparently and securely in a decentralized fashion has great potential to streamline the way we manage data in ways we could not have done so before.

Aside from the public blockchains used by cryptocurrencies, companies like Microsoft, IBM, and Amazon are developing their own blockchain services for use in the private sector. Companies like Walmart and Xbox have already deployed the blockchain to help improve their business, while even organizations like the United Nations are looking to blockchain-related technologies to help with humanitarian aid.

How Blockchain Works

When a Bitcoin transaction is made, the transaction is sent to a public ledger. This public ledger holds all of the unverified transactions on the network. A transaction will contain three things: The address of the wallet the bitcoin is coming from, the address of the wallet the bitcoin is going to, and the amount of bitcoin being moved. Until the transaction is verified and placed in a block in the blockchain, the transaction is not considered complete.

In order to verify a transaction, the transaction has to be taken by a miner, verified, and placed in a new block that is added to the blockchain. A block will contain a number of verified transactions based on its size and cryptographic hash that links the new block to the previous block in the chain. The process of creating a new block also confirms the integrity of the blocks in the chain that come before it. Due to this, the further back you go in the chain, the stronger the older blocks get, making them harder and harder to alter.

On the Bitcoin network, each computer running the Bitcoin software is called a node. Each node has a whole or partial copy of the blockchain as well as a copy of the ledger. When a miner successfully adds a new block to the blockchain, it is transmitted to all of the nodes on the network, so they can update their own blockchain and ledger.

The time it takes for a new block to be created is called the block time. Block time is determined by the size of the blockchain, the number of transactions needed to be verified based on the size of the block, and the amount of "work" necessary to find the new cryptographic hash.

Transaction time—the amount of time required to complete a transaction on the blockchain's network—is determined by the block time and how much traffic is going through the network, i.e., the number of transactions that must be verified. The more traffic on the network, the longer it will take for the transaction to be completed.

Bitcoin, for example, has a block size of 1 MB and an average block time of 10 minutes. This means that it will take roughly a minimum of 10 minutes for a transaction to complete. This time is also increased by the size of your transaction and the total amount of transactions waiting to be verified in the ledger. For example, on August 30th, 2021, the average confirmation time was 14.73 minutes, but two days later, on September 1st, it increased to 50.99 minutes (YCharts, 2021).

Strengths and Weaknesses of the Blockchain

All transactions on the blockchain are visible. Nothing in the blockchain or the public ledger is hidden, which means that anyone can look up a specific transaction. Once data has been added to the blockchain, it is almost impossible to alter. The decentralized nature of the blockchain also ensures that there is no singular point of failure in the network.

However, the decentralized nature of the blockchain network can also be a disadvantage to the system. In order for any meaningful change to the network to be made, one must have an overwhelming consensus from the network's community. This can be difficult to achieve sometimes. Failure to do so doesn't just cause rifts within the community, but those who refuse to follow through with the changes can cause the blockchain to fork.

The blockchain is also not as anonymous as some people might think. As previously mentioned, all transactions, both those in the blockchain and the public ledger, are visible to all, so anyone can look them up. Data is tracked by using a combination of addresses and public keys—both of which are generated by the private keys held by those who conduct transactions on the network. While one cannot be directly identified by their public key, if one were able to associate a specific person with a private key, one could easily keep track of their transactions and transaction history within the blockchain.

The other issue with public blockchains like Bitcoin is that they are inefficient. This was a feature rather than a bug, though. The proof-of-work system used by Bitcoin and most other altcoins currently in production is designed to help prevent hackers from taking over by making the mining process laborious. This has also had the side effect of having a negative impact on the environment, as Bitcoin operations require massive amounts of electricity in order to operate.

Forking

Forking occurs when two blocks are added to a chain at the same time—creating a split. This can have serious implications depending how and why the forking occurs.

The most common type of forking is when two miners create the next block in the chain at the same time. This creates a temporary fork in the blockchain. When this happens, the network's software determines which block is kept based on predetermined conditions. The winning block becomes the next block in the blockchain, while the losing block is orphaned and eventually discarded.

Soft forking occurs when something is done to change the network or software but does not change the composition of the blocks themselves. This could be a slight change to the rules on how blocks are made or a software patch. The result is a small difference in the blocks that are generated from that point on. However, the change is such that the older blocks in the chain do not perceive a difference in the new blocks, thus ensuring the continued integrity of the blockchain. Soft forks can also be temporary—only affecting a handful of blocks before the network returns to normal.

A hard fork is the opposite of a soft fork. Hard forking occurs when the rules or software change so drastically that the new blocks made are fundamentally different from the old blocks in the change. This results in the creation of a second, separate chain that is linked to the old chain at the time of forking. The most common cause of a hard fork is when one part of the network upgrades to a new software, while another part of the network keeps using the old software.

From the time of the forking, there will be two separate blockchains attached to the base chain. It will be the original chain that continues to be built up by those nodes who did not change and the new chain which is built up by the nodes that have. Each chain keeps a record of the old chain and its new chain while ignoring the other chain.

Generally, there are two reasons for hard forking. The first is to roll back the blockchain in order to erase blocks at the end of the chain. The Ethereum blockchain, for example, has had to do several hard forks in order to roll back token thefts on the network. Hard forking can also happen accidentally, such as when there is a bug in the software, or a certain number of nodes on the network do not update, causing two separate chains to be created.

Hard forking can also be the result of ideological divides within the network's community. If the community cannot agree on which direction to go, it can cause the two sides to split and go their separate ways. These types of hard forks often result in the creation of new altcoins.

Bitcoin Cash

One such example of a hard fork occurred with bitcoin. On August 1st, 2017, a hard fork occurred in the Bitcoin blockchain that created Bitcoin cash. The reason for the split was a disagreement within the Bitcoin community on how to improve transaction times. The group that ultimately created Bitcoin cash wanted to increase the individual block size from 1 MB to 8 MB so that more transactions could be held per block. This would allow for faster transaction time but would also increase the overall size of the blockchain to the point where it would be unsupportable on smaller computers (Frankenfield, 2021h).

Ethereum Classic

Another example of a hard fork occurred in Ethereum's blockchain. One of the organizations on Ethereum's Platform, called the DAO, was hacked by exploiting a weakness in the DAO's code. At the time of the hack in June 2016, the DAO had $50 million of its $150 million in tokens stolen. In the aftermath of the theft, the community debated doing a hard fork to rollback the theft and reappropriate the funds (Frankenfield, 2021h).

Suffice to say, the debate was a contentious one. There were many in the Ethereum community who believed that the theft should stand for better or worse. Eventually, the pro-forking side of the debate won out but not without consequence. When the fork occurred on July 30th, 2016, it created Ethereum classic, which continued the original, unforked Ethereum blockchain and a rivalry between the two groups that persists to this day.

Private Blockchains

Aside from the public blockchains, companies are also using the blockchain technology to their own advantages. Though the adoption of the blockchain in the private sector is still in the early stages, the few examples that have succeeded show that the blockchain has great potential to improve upon existing information structures and perhaps even the way we process data.

Unlike public blockchains, where the records are made public, private blockchains are permission specific. This generally means that records can only be added and not altered, and only specific nodes on the network are allowed to mine new blocks. Public blockchains are also trustless, meaning that everything must be verified including the blockchain. Private blockchains work the opposite way, with nodes accessing the blockchain already considered to be trusted.

Private blockchains are not as decentralized as public ones. While a private network may have a number of nodes, they are still ultimately under the control of a single entity. Private blockchains also tend to be smaller than public blockchains, making them potentially easier to be hijacked by a 51% attack (more on the 51% attack in the next chapter).

However, private blockchains tend to be much more efficient than public ones. They are also easier to scale and upgrade, and there is almost no anonymity on a private blockchain network as there is on a public one. Being smaller, private blockchains also tend to process transactions faster and require far less overhead than a public blockchains.

FedEx

As one of the largest logistics management companies in the world, FedEx currently uses blockchain to track their high value cargo. Aside from expanding to cover all of their cargo with blockchain, FedEx is also pioneering the development of blockchain-based supply chain logistics standards for the industry.

Walmart

In order to help track E. coli outbreaks and other issues, Walmart implemented its own private blockchain in order to track its produce. Suppliers upload certificates of authenticity and other data to the blockchain, which can quickly be used to track shipments of produce from the store back to their source. A process that in the past could take days now takes only minutes, and it brings a new level of trust and certainty to the safety of Walmart's produce.

The United Nations

In order to keep up with its mandate, the United Nations (UN) has been quick to embrace new technologies to help its humanitarian efforts. During the Syrian refugee crisis, the UN in 2017 implemented the blockchain to help manage and distribute funds to refugees in Jordan's Azraq refugee camp. Instead of using ID cards which could be stolen or prepaid credit cards which have large overhead costs, the UN used a blockchain and retinal scans.

Refugees were credited funds, which are stored on the blockchain. When the refugee goes to buy something, they use an iris scanner to prove their identity, and a transaction occurs on the blockchain that pays for their purchase. This not only cut down on overhead costs but also prevented the system from being exploited by warlords or other bad actors who would in the past steal ID or credit cards from refugees (Juskalian, 2018).

Xbox

In order to help cut down on its paperwork, Xbox implemented a private blockchain to help reduce its accounting overhead. Working in conjunction with Microsoft and EY, Xbox created a private blockchain run by smart contracts that manages gaming rights and royalty payments.

Chapter 3:

Crypto Mining

Mining is where the work of the blockchain is done. As we've already explained, miners create new blocks by validating transactions and adding them to the blockchain. Each time a new block is mined, the entire blockchain's integrity is verified, ensuring consistency. With every new block that is added to the blockchain, new coins are created as a reward for the miner who created the block.

Yet mining blocks is not that simple. In order to successfully mine a block, you must put the work in.

Proof-of-Work System

Bitcoin and most cryptocurrencies use proof-of-work systems to produce new blocks in the blockchain. In order to create the next block in the chain, a miner has to do two things: validate a number of transactions and find the next cryptographic hash.

Validating transactions is done through consensus. In order for a transaction to be considered valid, the majority of the network must see the transaction as being valid by comparing it to the one in their own public ledger. Once a transaction is validated, it is added to the block. Once the block is filled with validated transactions, the miner must now complete a mathematical equation to try and find the next cryptographic hash in the chain.

Finding the next hash number is not an easy task. Proof-of-work was designed in such a way that it would help make the process more secure by making finding the next hash number difficult and time consuming. Not anyone can just mine blocks. If you do not have the necessary computing power to compete with other miners, you will not find the next hash number. This helps ensure that not anyone can just come along and tamper with the blockchain.

The hashing function takes the previous cryptographic hash, the verified transactions, and a number called the nonce to try and create the new hash number. The correct hash number will have the correct number of leading zeros. If the calculation comes up with the wrong number, it keeps repeating the process until the right one is found. If another miner finds the correct hash number first, the other miners have to restart the block creation process from scratch.

Finding that correct number is, for the most part, purely guesswork. Not only that, but the difficulty of finding the right hash number increases or decreases based on the number of miners that are currently working.

The Rewards of Mining

The miner who successfully mines the next block in the chain receives a fixed number of coins. In order to ensure scarcity, all cryptos are designed so that they will only ever produce a certain number of coins. This reward dwindles over time at regular intervals. For Bitcoin, the reward for mining new blocks halves every four years. When Bitcoin first started, the reward was 50 coins per block mined. Currently, the reward is set at 6.25 coins per block mined. By the time the reward reaches zero, the last reward block will be mined roughly sometime in 2140.

However, miners are not just paid by finding the new block. Each transaction on the network has a fee associated with it. When a miner mines a new block, they not only get the reward for mining the block but all of the transaction fees that came with the individual transactions they verified.

Transaction fees are determined by a combination of network congestion and the size of the transaction. The larger your transaction, the more space it needs in the block, which means less transactions getting added to the block. Likewise, the busier the network is, the longer it can take for a transaction to be validated and added to the block. Giving your transaction a higher transaction fee will give the miner more incentive to process your transaction first before the lower one.

Mining Rigs

Gone are the days when you could mine Bitcoin with your trusty desktop or laptop. Due to the length of the Bitcoin blockchain and the complexity of the hash function, finding the right hash number could take a standard computer decades or even centuries.

While one can still mine some altcoins with their personal computer, older coins like Bitcoin require more processing power. Since you are competing with other miners to find the next hash number first, you need to be able to calculate the hash faster than they do. Rather than use regular computers, miners use specialized computers known as mining rigs.

Mining rigs measure their computational power by the number of hashes they can calculate in a second (h/s).

Hash Name	# of Hashes per second	Abbreviation
Kilo Hash	1000	kH/s*
Mega Hash	1,000,000	MH/s
Giga Hash	1,000,000,000	GH/s
Tera Hash	1,000,000,000,000	TH/s
Peta Hash	1,000,000,000,000,000	PH/s
Exa Hash	1,000,000,000,000,000,000	EH/s
Zeta Hash	1,000,000,000,000,000,000,000	ZH/s
Yotta Hash	1,000,000,000,000,000,000,000,000	YH/s

*kH/s is always written with a lower case k so as not to be confused with Kelvins (K)

Individually, most mining rigs measure in the GH/s to TH/s range, with some low-end models running in the MH/s range. However, serious mining operations can run dozens upon dozens of rights linked together in a single network to pool their hashing power together.

Suffice to say, the standard computer CPU is not going to be able to keep up with this type of work. Due to this, most miners use either Application Specific Integrated Circuits (ASICs), or Graphical Processor Units (GPUs).

ASICs

ASICs are specialized chips designed to do one task and one task only. They are generally used for specific purposes and can be found in digital recorders, communication equipment, cars, and smartphones. Mining ASICS are designed for the mining of new blocks—particularly the calculating of the new hash number.

Mining ASICs come in dedicated computers, or rigs, and are quite expensive. Low-end models range around $2,000, while higher end units can go for up to $10,000 or more.

GPUs

Prior to the creation of the mining ASICs, the GPUs found in computer graphics cards were the go-to processors for mining. While it is pretty much impossible to mine bitcoins with GPUs these days, GPU-based mining rigs can be used to mine a number of altcoins.

GPU-powered rigs are still used by low-end miners and those who dabble in crypto mining. Also, companies like NVIDIA have also begun developing mining-dedicated GPUs for mining Ethereum and other altcoin.

The Cost of Mining

As we've already shown, in order to mine a block, you need to come up with the next hash number first. In order to do that, you need to have more hash power than the other miners—more is the keyword. Most serious miners will not have a single mining rig but multiple and maybe even dozens. Large mining operations can have hundreds or even thousands of mining rigs working together to get hash power extremely high H/s. However, all this hashing power comes at a cost.

Mining rigs are not conservative when it comes to power consumption. Most current mining rights draw 1000+ watts of electricity, and some high-end rigs can draw 3000+ watts of electricity. To put that in perspective, a standard computer desktop power supply draws 300 to 500 watts, with high-end ones going into the range of 600 to 800 watts. Power supplies in the 1000+ watt range are generally only needed in very high-end custom computers.

As a result, mining operations, even small ones, use large amounts of electricity. It's estimated that Bitcoin mining uses approximately 129.24 terawatts per hour (TWH) per year (Energyrates, 2021). This is as much or more electricity than some small countries use in a year and is only for Bitcoin mining. The total amount of electricity used for the mining of all altcoins would be much higher.

Due to this energy requirement, most mining operations occur in parts of the world where electricity is cheap and plentiful. Even then, some jurisdictions are not welcoming to crypto miners. With the state of environment also becoming a more prevalent issue, crypto mining is also not being viewed in the best light.

Solo Mining vs. Mining Pools

These days, getting the hash power needed to be a competitive miner requires a significant start-up investment. However, that number will vary depending on which cryptocurrency you are trying to mine. Since older currencies have large hashes, they require more hash power to solve. Older currencies like Bitcoin also already have a large, well-established community of miners, making getting in potentially that much harder. Since hash power is so key in mining the next block, a number of miners have banded together to form mining pools.

Mining pools take the hashing powers of all the rigs within their network and combine them to more quickly calculate the correct hash. The pool's software manages the efforts of the individual pool members and rewards them based on their share of the work accepted by the pool.

As technology continues to produce better mining rigs and the calculations become longer and longer, solo mining bitcoins and some other cryptos is becoming more difficult to do profitably. Even with newer altcoins, solo miners can easily be outpaced by better armed competitors or pools. While it is still possible to turn a profit as a solo miner with some altcoins, most individual miners end up joining mining pools.

Is Mining Worth It?

Generally, it's not recommended to start crypto mining. Compared to investing in crypto by buying and selling bitcoins and other altcoins, crypto mining requires a much larger initial investment in order to get started. Though the amount of this initial investment will vary depending on which coin you chose to mine, you will still need, at the very least, an above-average computer in order to be competitive.

The other issue with mining is that if the electrical rates in your area are too high, they will cut into any potential profit you might make. This holds particularly true if you plan on starting a large mining operation. You will need to be in a location with electrical rates as low as $0.10 USD/kWh or lower (Energyrates, 2021). Otherwise, high-energy costs will eat into your profits.

Proof-of-Stake

As we've shown, the proof-of-work method of crypto mining is very inefficient. While the proof-of-work design does help to prevent tampering with the blockchain, it requires large amounts of processing power in order to mine the next block in the chain and even more power to be the first one to do it. However, a new form of crypto mining, proof-of-stake, is slowly emerging.

In the proof-of-stake model, miners stake some of their own coins. The amount of coins the miner stakes determines the total number of transactions they can validate. The miner to validate the next block in the chain is picked at random. The more coins a miner has staked, the more likely they are to get picked. Instead of getting a block reward, miners would get a network fee as their reward.

Coins staked in this way cannot be spent while staked. Furthermore, if the miner tries to somehow cheat the system by providing false data or bad blocks, they won't only be banned from the network but also lose some of their staked coins as a penalty.

Ethereum will be upgrading to proof-of-stake with its Ethereum 2.0, while some other coins, like Cardano and NXT, already use proof-of-stake.

Advantages and Disadvantages of Proof-of-Stake

Unlike proof-of-work, whose success is ultimately determined by the amount of hash power at your disposal, proof-of-stake is seen as being proportional and fair. The amount of coins you stake will dictate how likely you are to mine the next block, and even if you stake only a small number of coins, you will see some profit. The more coins you stake, the more fees you will collect. This is in sharp contrast to the proof-of-work model, where you must not only pay the initial investment but keep investing in new technology to ensure your hash power stays competitive.

Proof-of-stake would also be much more efficient than proof-of-work in processing transactions. Staking would also reduce the electrical and environmental costs of crypto mining.

However, proof-of-stake is still untested, with some believing that it will not work. There is also the potential threat of centralization, where a few wealthy individuals could stake enough coins to gain a majority within the network.

The 51% Attack

As mentioned in the previous chapter, trying to hack Bitcoin and the blockchain is next to impossible because of its very nature. However, the blockchain's security is not flawless. If one were to control enough of the network so that they are the ones creating the new blocks, they could provide falsified transactions that would then be added to the blockchain. This would allow them to halt payments or even reverse transactions to double-spend their coins.

This type of attack, known as the 51% attack, would require the attacker to control 51% of the total network, so they would have enough power to generate the next block in the chain before anyone else.

- In a proof-of-work network like Bitcoin, a 51% attack would require the attacker to control at least 51% of the total mining hash power.

- In a proof-of-stake network like Ethereum 2.0, one would have to control 51% or more of the total staked coins.

As you might guess, controlling 51% of either hash power or staked coins is no simple matter. The more nodes in the network, or the more coins in circulation, would make it increasingly harder and more costly to wage such an attack. While a 51% attack is not likely to happen to larger cryptos like Bitcoin and Ethereum, it has happened to smaller Bitcoin Gold Blockchain as well as Krypton and Shift—two blockchains based on Ethereum's blockchain.

Cloud Mining

Cloud mining operations are crypto mining farms where the owner of the farm sells or leases its hash power. Similar to the cloud that stores data, cloud mining allows a miner to take part in mining without having to purchase or maintain any of the hardware necessary to mining with.

The idea behind cloud mining is that the prospective miners pay a fee or invest into the operation. The miner contracts a certain amount of the network's hash power for a certain amount of time. The miner then receives a reward based proportionally on the amount of hash power they have contracted. The more money the miner invests and the longer they stay, the more rewards they will see.

Cloud mining provides a simple, hands-off means for one to benefit from crypto mining. Unfortunately, while there are some legitimate cloud mining services out there, most are either scams designed to steal your money or do not last long enough to turn a profit. Even within a legitimate cloud mining service, it's possible you could still lose money if the service is not profitable during the tenure of your contract.

Again, while there are legitimate cloud mining services out there, our recommendation is to avoid them. Cloud mining is a very risky endeavor, and should you choose to try any of these services, make sure you do your due diligence and thoroughly research the service before signing up.

Cryptojacking

Cryptojacking is a process where malware is installed on a computer system and used to mine cryptocurrency. This is done by hijacking the computer's resources and turning them to mining. Using a network of jacked computer systems, hackers mine crypto and receive the rewards.

Since crypto mining is very processing intensive, cryptojacking can cause computer systems to heat up and wear out a lot quicker. The malware can even be installed on phones but can cause the phone to heat up and potentially cause permanent damage to it.

Cryptojacking is relatively rare, but it still does happen. It appeals to many hackers and cyber criminals because it is easy to set up and deploy and has little risk for the hacker. Fortunately, like all malware and viruses, security experts are continually watching for new cryptojacking attempts. Cryptojacking itself is no worse threat than most other viruses or malware, so as long as one keeps up safe computer habits, one does not need to worry about this threat.

Chapter 4:

The Currency of the Future

Since its creation, Bitcoin has slowly been gaining popularity beyond the niche groups where it first started. Though it's been little over a decade since its inception, we have barely scratched the surface in terms of what cryptocurrency and the blockchain has to offer. However, it will still be quite a while before we see crypto and the blockchain's full potential being realized.

Bitcoin's Volatility and Trouble With Authority

Bitcoin's value is purely speculative. It is not pegged to any fiat currency or asset nor is it supported by any government or financial institution. As such, its value is determined almost solely by the amount of publicity and the demand there is for the coins. It's because of this that even a single story or even a single tweet can cause the price to rise or fall. However, despite the various crashes Bitcoin has suffered over the years, the value of the coin continues to steadily rise.

Part of the reason for Bitcoin's recent popularity and rise is the number of big names and companies that have begun to invest in Bitcoin and related technologies. PayPal, for example, opened up its platform in 2020 to allow the buying, selling, holding, and even paying for purchases through their platform with Bitcoin, Ethereum, Litecoin, and Bitcoin Cash. Meanwhile, companies like Tesla and Square One have invested millions in acquiring bitcoin, while firms like J.P. Morgan and Signature Bank are also investing in crypto.

However, while investors and businesses are warming up to cryptocurrencies, governments are moving much slower. Some countries, like Egypt, Nigeria, and Turkey have even gone so far as to ban their banking sectors from dealing in Bitcoin or other altcoins. Even in more developed Western countries, cryptocurrency is not viewed favorably. While some would point to its potential for being used in money laundering, or its volatility making it a poor asset, a large part of the reason for the dislike toward crypto is the lack of control.

As we previously mentioned, Bitcoin was designed to be decentralized and beyond the ability for any one government or institution to control. The blockchain is also very transparent, with little in the way of secrecy. It was these points and others that drew many of the original Bitcoin and crypto enthusiasts. Some even held the more extreme views of Bitcoin as a means of going so far as to disrupt or even destroy the traditional banking systems. This will likely never happen.

Governments rely on their fiat currencies to help manage their economies. Money policy is one of the major parts of keeping a country's economic wheels greased. If something goes wrong in the economy, a country's central bank can either buy up or print more of their fiat currency to help solve the problem. This, however, doesn't always work, but it is nonetheless a tool governments around the world rely on to help keep their economy stable.

While it is clear that cryptocurrencies are not going away right now, how exactly they will fit into the global economy is still to be seen. Currently, Bitcoin is being treated more as an asset than as a currency by large institutions. Even now, altcoins like Litecoin and Bitcoin Cash are trying to step up and replace Bitcoin as the preferred spending crypto. Part of how things will turn out will be determined in part by how governments chose to regulate cryptocurrency.

Tokenizing Fiat Currencies

The odds of a government adopting Bitcoin or any cryptocurrency in place of their fiat currency are astronomically low. To date, only one country, El Salvador, recognizes Bitcoin as legal tender. While others might follow suit, this is not expected to happen in the near future. The fact is cryptocurrency and their decentralized networks offer no real advantages for governments.

Rather than adopting a cryptocurrency as their own, governments are more likely to tokenize their fiat currency into a digital one. In this scenario, a government would deploy its own blockchain and crypto and peg it to their fiat currency. The government would then encourage the use of its digital currency for online transactions, and over time, this would allow them to compete with cryptos in the digital currency markets.

In this scenario, the government would benefit from the blockchain and cryptocurrency, while retaining control over the crypto itself. The blockchain network would be run much like a private blockchain, with government systems or trusted companies acting as the nodes to validate transactions and mine blocks in the chain. Meanwhile, vendors would accept the currency as payment without fear of volatile price swings because it is pegged to the government's fiat currency.

This scenario is not as far-fetched as some might think. In fact, it's already starting to happen.

China and the Digital Yuan

In 2014, the People's Bank of China began researching digital currency. By 2017, the development of a new digital currency had begun. In 2019, the Digital Currency Electronic Payment (DCEP) system was announced. Soon after, trials of the new digital currency and payment system were rolled out; on August 9th, 2021, China began sales of their YuanPay Group coin (Bram, 2021).

Prior to the release of the digital yuan, Chinese authorities had been cracking down on the use of Bitcoin and other altcoins within their jurisdiction, including shutting down Ant Financial's IPO In November of 2020. This helped pave the way for their own coin when it was eventually released.

According to the People's Bank of China, DCEP was designed to help counter the influence of Bitcoin and other altcoins on the Chinese market. DCEP was also designed to streamline digital payment within China and perhaps eventually beyond. It could also serve to cut down on fraud and other financial crimes, though the digital yuan is not without its detractors (Bram, 2021).

Many have pointed out that the use of the digital yuan would give Chinese authorities a new tool with which to monitor their citizens via their transactions. Despite Chinese authorities claiming the contrary, some economists also fear that China's new digital currency could be used to challenge and maybe even destabilize the American dollar as the primary global reserve currency.

While the digital yuan seems to be doing well in China, it's still too early to tell how the coin will do on the world stage. Part of this will also depend on how other countries react to the new coin, but the fact that China is so far ahead of other major countries in the area of digital currency has not gone unnoticed and may very well be something to be concerned about.

Facebook's Diem (Formerly Facebook Libra)

In China, WeChat—one of the most used apps in China—is a multiuse platform: It not only serves as a messaging and social media app but also has a built-in digital wallet known as WeChat Pay that users can use to pay bills, transfer money, and make purchases with their mobile at locations that support WeChat Pay. Coupled with some other features, WeChat is the one app that can do almost everything while within China's borders.

Seeing the success of WeChat, it is unsurprising that Facebook would try to follow suit. However, Facebook is taking it one step further by creating their own cryptocurrency, the Libra, which was later renamed to Diem due to legal issues with the name.

Facebook's Diem project isn't just about creating a new crypto: It plans to create an entire financial network. Its primary goal is to make international money transfers quicker and simpler, which would be a great step up from the current system where sending money abroad can take weeks to accomplish and can be fairly expensive.

To do this, Facebook's Diem project will use its own stablecoin, the Diem, and will run on a private blockchain. Facebook will support the diem with a reverse basket of fiat currencies consisting primarily of American dollars and a mix of other fiats.

To help oversee the project, Facebook established the Libra Association (later renamed to the Diem Association) in Geneva, Switzerland. The association comprises a number of venture capitalists, nonprofits, companies, and blockchain-related groups.

The project, however, has not been without its issues. Before the first meeting of the Libra Association, a number of its original members, including eBay, PayPal, Mastercard, and Visa, left the association. Various governments, including the United States, have also had a lukewarm reception to the original announcement.

Aside from potential monopoly and antitrust issues, one of the larger concerns about the Diem project is privacy. Facebook would, in theory, have access to the transaction history of their users who use the Diem crypto and network and could use that data for their own purposes or to even sell to other companies. The other issue that Facebook faces with Diem is that it puts the company into a position that is very similar in ways to a bank; it has been suggested that if they want to start acting like a bank, they will have to be treated as such and forced to comply with banking regulations.

Despite the opposition from various governments, central banks, and privacy groups, Diem's development is still ongoing. Diem is scheduled to release a pilot event sometime in 2021, though it is fairly likely that this will be pushed back to 2022. Given the broad resistance the project is facing, it will be interesting to see if Diem makes it out of development and into production. If it does manage to do so, we suspect that it will have to go through some changes in order to meet scrutiny and take additional steps to go above regulatory compliance in order to be accepted.

Chapter 5:

Which Cryptocurrencies to

Watch and Invest In

At the time of writing, according to CoinMarketCap (2021), there are 11,496 cryptocurrencies available across 397 exchanges. Of these coins, CoinMarketCap is tracking the price of 6,239 of them. As time goes on, the odds are very good that these numbers will continue to rise.

This leaves one with the interesting, and perhaps a little mind-boggling, question of figuring out which coins will be worth investing in. Fortunately, we will be answering that question right now.

Author's Note: The following prices were referenced from the website coinmarketcap.com at the time of writing and are subject to change.

Bitcoin (BTC) Is Still at the Top

With its current price ranging between $47,0000 and $49,000, Bitcoin (BTC) is still at the top of the cryptocurrency charts. While Wrapped Bitcoin (WBTC) and Bitcoin BEP2 (BTCB) are about even (WBTC at the time of writing is about $100 ahead of BTC), I doubt most people would have heard of either of these altcoins. This is hardly surprising.

When one talks about cryptocurrency in general, Bitcoin is the one coin literally everyone has heard about. As the original cryptocurrency, Bitcoin is the oldest and still the most popular. Whether it is still the best coin is a debate that could be had but not one we will be discussing in this book.

In terms of investment value, Bitcoin is still expected to continue to rise in price and popularity as time goes on.

"Spending" Type Altcoins

One of Bitcoin's largest deficiencies is its transaction times. As we talked about in Chapter 2, Bitcoin's average block time is 10 minutes. This means that if you go into a store and try to buy something with Bitcoin, it will take around 10 minutes at minimum before the transaction either comes back as being completed or cancelled. If you are a merchant, this would be a reason not to want to accept Bitcoin as a form of payment. However, where Bitcoin fails, other altcoins have taken up the slack (YCharts, 2021).

Bitcoin Cash (BCH)

As we talked about, Bitcoin Cash was created as a result of a hard fork in the bitcoin blockchain when part of the bitcoin community wanted to increase the size of the blocks to 8 MB. They also did away with the recent segregated witness (SegWit) upgrade that Bitcoin adopted before the hard fork.

Bitcoin Cash is the earliest example of a currency created by a hard fork to remain successful. Its size and implementation allows for faster transaction speeds, which is generally better than Bitcoin's own. However, Bitcoin Cash has yet to live up to its potential and has itself seen a hard fork, creating Bitcoin SV. At the time of writing, Bitcoin Cash's value is around $650. Despite its troubles, Bitcoin Cash is still seen as a viable alternative to Bitcoin and is accepted in places and by companies that accept altcoins.

Litecoin (LTC)

Litecoin was created by former Google engineer Charles Lee back in 2001 and was one of the first altcoins created. It has a faster block time compared to Bitcoin at 2.5 minutes, and as a result, it has much faster transaction times. However, its proof-of-work method is more complicated and requires more specialized hardware to mine than Bitcoin.

Currently, Litecoin has a value of around $180 and has a growing number of merchants who accept it.

Should I Get Them?

Both of these altcoins show value as a spending type of crypto rather than an investing type of crypto. Since they are also much cheaper, if you are looking for a coin to strictly spend, these might be cheaper alternatives to Bitcoin. However, most places that accept Bitcoin Cash and Litecoin also accept Bitcoin. Due to this, we neither encourage nor discourage the use of these coins.

Ethereum (ETH)

If you were to ask most investors and analysts, they would probably tell you that Bitcoin is the only cryptocurrency worth investing in. While true from a purely financial standpoint, there is one other competitor that is worth talking about.

Since the creation of Bitcoin in 2009, Ethereum is so far the only altcoin that almost managed to upstage Bitcoin from its top position—and with good reason. While Bitcoin is a strong digital currency, it did not come with any tools or code to help develop the apps and programs necessary to actually use it. Those were slowly developed over time by other programmers who wanted to take part in what Bitcoin has to offer. Ethereum sought to change that.

Unlike Bitcoin, Ethereum is not simply a digital currency. Ethereum is a development platform complete with its own scripting language designed not only to provide an altcoin in the form of its ether but also the means with which to build applications and systems that can leverage the power of crypto.

Smart Contracts

Perhaps Ethereum's biggest contribution to the blockchain is the smart contracts. Smart contracts are programs or protocols that are designed to carry out a transaction on the blockchain once certain requirements are met. They are, in a sense, like digital vending machines: You put something, like money, into a smart contract, and something predictable comes out of it.

Smart contracts allow for the automation of transactions and have a list of potential uses, such as in auctions, insurance, gambling, voting, or even paying people, as we saw with Xbox. Smart contracts are also secure: Once they start, they cannot be stopped. At the same time, smart contracts are also open-source software, meaning anyone can look at the code that will be executed.

Decentralized Apps (dApps) and Decentralized Financing (DeFi)

By using smart contracts and some other code, one can build programs and applications on Ethereum's platform that can do a host of things. These decentralized apps run on the Ethereum network and use Ethereum's blockchain to store data. With dApps, it can be anything from games to online gambling and even financial programs. The dApps are also the backbone of a Decentralized Financial (DeFi) system.

The idea behind DeFi is to have a financial system that is completely separate from traditional control mechanisms of business and government. DeFi systems consist of a number of dApps that can be used to carry out complex financial services, including loans; trading cryptocurrencies and tokens; or even earning interest in savings-like accounts.

To support DeFi apps and systems, Ethereum allows for the creation of tokens which dApps can use as a currency within the Ethereum platform.

Is It Worth Getting?

Currently, Ethereum's ether, the name of its coin, is worth roughly $3,800—a far cry from Bitcoin's current price.

However, Ethereum has consistently been the second most popular crypto available, with a market cap second only to Bitcoin. The real difference, however, is what Ethereum offers in the form of its development platform.

While companies have been buying and adding Bitcoin to their portfolios due to its rising value and popularity, large companies like Alphabet—the parent company of Google—Square One, and Tesla have also taken an interest in Ethereum, particularly with its recent efforts to reduce its carbon footprint by moving from proof-of-work to proof-of-stake.

While perhaps not as lucrative as Bitcoin, Ethereum is a solid performer, and unlike Bitcoin, its value is not just based on hype. Ethereum's platform has much to offer, and we suspect that it may last longer than Bitcoin.

Cardano (ADA)

If one talks about Ethereum, one must also talk about its competitor, Cardano. Cardano uses the ADA as its cryptocurrency.

A new altcoin that only saw its first stable release on May 13th 2021, Cardano was founded in 2015 by one of the original co-founders of Ethereum, Charles Hoskinson. Hoskinson left Ethereum to create Cardano after a falling out with another of Ethereum's original founders, Vitalik Buterin. Hoskinson wanted Ethereum to accept venture capital and eventually become a for-profit entity. Buterin refused, and Hoskinson eventually went his own way, creating his own company, IOHK, and the Cardano Foundation (Wikipedia Foundation, 2021f).

Cardano is essentially an upgraded version of Ethereum. Like Ethereum, it is a full platform on which one can develop smart contracts and dApps, using a specialized smart contract language developed for the platform. It has been using proof-of-stake from its inception, and its design also resolves some of the scalability issues faced by other cryptocurrencies, while at the same time remaining in more regulatory compliance.

Some view Cardano as Ethereum's replacement, but whether that will be the case very much remains to be seen. As mentioned in the previous section, Ethereum is still evolving, with Ethereum 2.0 slowly being rolled out at the time of writing, so it can still potentially stay ahead of Cardano development-wise. Cardano itself is still very much in its infancy but has already secured a number of technology contracts with Ethiopia.

At the moment, Cardano's ADA is trading at $2.82. It's not worth investing in, but Cardano is definitely a crypto to watch in the coming years as it continues to grow.

Stablecoins

Stablecoins are a subset of crypto that are pegged to a fiat currency or asset. The idea behind stablecoins is that the issuers of the coins will be holding an equal amount of the fiat or asset it is pegged at, so if necessary, the coins can be redeemed for the pegged commodity at a 1:1 ratio. This gives the crypto a stability that prevents its price from dropping below the value of the pegged commodity.

Stablecoins are essentially the middle ground between traditional cryptos like Bitcoin and Ethereum, as well as the tokenized currencies discussed in the previous chapter. Stablecoins have all the trappings of a public blockchain but are also backed by a commodity that gives them stability and confidence that other cryptos do not have.

Most stablecoins pegged to a fiat currency use the USD. Digital Gold (DGX) is a stablecoin that is pegged to the price of gold. A few other stablecoins, like the DAI, use Ethereum or other cryptocurrencies to back itself.

Tether (USDT)

Tether is currently the most popular stablecoin available. Tether is pegged to the American dollar but also has versions of itself pegged to the euro and the Japanese yen. This ensures its price remains stable at all times. Tether is currently worth $1.

However, Tether has not been without controversy. In 2018, Tether ran afoul of regulators. Its lack of transparency also led to accusations by the New York Attorney General Letitia James that the parent company of Tether, IFinex Inc., was hiding an $850 million loss. This has led to questions of whether or not Tether has enough cash or commodity reserves to fully back their coin (Lopatto, 2021).

At the time of writing, the controversies surrounding Tether have yet to be fully resolved. If Tether should fall, it could have big, lasting consequences for the cryptocurrency industry in general. For now, it may be best to avoid Tether until it resolves its current legal woes.

Dogecoin (DOGE)

Before we get into the details of this coin, let us firmly state that we do not recommend that you invest in Dogecoin. Currently, Dogecoin has a value of roughly 30¢ and will likely never go above $1.

Dogecoin was originally released on December 6th, 2013, by software engineers Billy Markus and Jackson Palmer. Dogecoin was released as a joke, with its name and logo based on a popular dog meme at the time. Unlike other cryptocurrencies, Dogecoin was never meant to be taken seriously and was originally made as a jab to Bitcoin's price volatility.

However, joking aside, Dogecoin found a niche among Reddit and Twitter users, and thanks to some high-profile names touting the coin, including Elon Musk and Snoop Dogg, Dogecoin has gained some popularity. It was also adopted by the Dallas Mavericks basketball team as a means to purchase tickets and merchandise. Mark Cuban, the owner of the Mavericks, has also tweeted that Dogecoin could be a fun way to teach young people about investing in crypto (Vasic, 2021b).

However, aside from its status as a joke and poor investment vehicle, the coin itself has some issues. Dogecoin has stated that it will supply 100 billion coins. Bitcoin will only ever produce 21 million coins. There is also no implemented hard cap on Dogecoin's production, meaning that coins will be generated infinitely. The current block reward for Dogecoin is 10,000 coins. Before this was set on March 14th, 2014, the block reward was randomized (Wikipedia Foundation, 2021n).

Dogecoin will most likely continue to make the news from time to time, particularly since Elon Musk, the founder of Tesla, seems to have taken an interest in it. However, we cannot stress enough that Dogecoin was never meant to be, and still isn't, taken seriously as a cryptocurrency. As such, it's not recommended that you invest in this coin.

Getting Into Crypto on the Ground Floor

When a new company wants to raise funds, they often put out an Initial Public Offering (IPO). When someone wants to start a new altcoin, related app, or service and needs to raise funds, they can do something similar called an Initial Coin Offering (ICO).

When an ICO is started, the start-up usually publishes a white paper outlining the project and their goal. They then go about fundraising, exchanging fiat currency (or tokens) for the new altcoins they will be producing. These tokens can be utility tokens that are exchanged for some service once the project is up and running. They can also be security tokens that could be used to indicate how much stake a holder has in the project.

Most ICOs Are Scams

It doesn't take much to start an ICO, and they are, for the most part, unregulated. Due to this, most ICOs end up being scams designed to cheat investors out of their money. That does not mean all ICOs are scams: Valid ICOs also exist and tend to be easier to identify if one does their research.

BitConnect

One of the largest ICO scams, BitConnect was touted as being a high-yield investment program that was in reality a Ponzi scheme. Released in 2016, BitConnect ran until it was shut down on January 16th, 2018. During the time it operated, BitConnect managed to defraud its investors of more than two billion dollars in the United States alone.

BitConnect was billed as a lending platform where users traded Bitcoin for BitConnect coin. These coins could be invested in the BitConnect platform where they would earn daily interest. Once the investment term was completed, the user would regain their lended coin to either take out or reinvest back into the platform. Interest payouts would be handled by a "trading bot" and "volatility software" which would calculate how much interest you would get.

In actuality, BitConnect was a sham, where earlier investors were paid by money taken from newer investors. When the platform was shut down in 2018, the price of its coin also plummeted—further adding to the losses already incurred by the scheme.

Currently, the SEC is trying to sue BitConnect's founder, Satish Kumbhani, an Indian citizen, for the fraud in order to impose fines and to recoup some of the two billion dollars lost. Glenn Arcaro, the primary promoter of BitConnect in the United States, along with several other BitConnect promoters, have also been charged. Arcaro has already pleaded guilty to related criminal charges (Stempel, 2021).

How to Identify Fraudulent ICOs

As you can see from the BitConnect example, fraudsters can swindle investors for large amounts of money. In BitConnect's case, investors were guaranteed up to 40% returns on their investment. This alone should have been a warning sign that something wasn't right. BitConnect's use of a so-called trading bot and volatility software should also have been a warning sign that something was not right with the platform. However, not all fraudulent ICOs have such clear warning signs.

It's not recommended that you invest in ICOs. If you do decide to invest in an ICO, make sure you do your due diligence in determining not only if the ICO is fraudulent but also if it is one that might actually succeed. Most non-fraudulent ICOs do not succeed. That is in large part because these ICOs are often fueled by hype and/or were poorly designed and destined to fail.

The first test in determining if an ICO is a fraud or not is by examining its white paper. An ICO's white paper will not only outline the planned goals for the project but its strategies, concerns, and timeline. A white paper will tell you if the company's concepts are sound and competitive. They should also offer supporting resources, including financial models, legal concerns, SWOT analysis, and a roadmap for implementation (Reiff, 2021b). If the ICO has no white paper or the white paper does not give you confidence that the project will succeed, then you should avoid that ICO.

Getting to know the people involved in the ICO, from the administrators to the developers, will also help to identify fraudulent ICOs as well. While you do not need to research every name involved, identifying the key personnel in an ICO and their backgrounds and experience in relation to the project will help you better judge if the ICO will succeed. Likewise, if the staff is too small for the scope of the project or the people involved have little information attached to them, that is a warning sign that the ICO should be avoided.

Token or coin sales can also be key in telling the difference between a fraudulent or bona fide ICO. Legitimate ICOs will have the infrastructure in place to make acquiring their token or coin offerings easy. They will also not hesitate to show the progress of their sales. Fraudulent ICOs, on the other hand, or even those poorly managed ones, will not have sales information readily available and will even obfuscate their sales numbers. Their token might also be more difficult to acquire, though that is not always the case.

Lastly, and perhaps more importantly, do not fall for any of the hype that might be associated with an ICO. If it seems like it may be a get-rich-quick scheme, it may be just that. Speculators can also inflate the value of an ICO, so they can make a profit off the ICO even if it fails. Rather than buy into the hype, do your due diligence to make sure the ICO is worthy of the hype it is receiving.

Again, don't invest in ICOs. Rather than investing in an ICO, an STO would be a better investment vehicle.

Security Token Offering (STO)

In 2017, the SEC cracked down on ICOs in the United States, eventually banning them altogether. If one wants to do an ICO in America, they need to instead do a Security Token Offering (STO).

An STO is a regulated form of ICO where the start-up has to go through one of several different regulations in order to be able to offer their tokens to potential investors. This ensures to some degree that the start-up is not trying to run a fraud. However, running through these regulatory hoops can be cumbersome, but if one wants to raise funds from American investors, the STO is the only way to legally do so.

At the time of writing, most developed countries support some form of STOs. While ICOs are not banned in all places like they are in the United States, there is a possibility that they will be eventually. Currently, aside from the United States, China and South Korea have banned ICOs. China and South Korea have also banned STOs.

Unlike ICOs, investing in STOs is a good option. However, even though STOs are more regulated, there's no guarantee that they will ultimately be successful. If you do want to invest in an STO, follow the steps outlined in the previous section to help you determine if the STO has a chance at succeeding.

Chapter 6:

Crypto Wallets

Buying Bitcoin or other cryptos is relatively easy. The one thing you will need for the process is a crypto wallet. Unlike physical wallets, crypto wallets are not actually used to store your coins. Rather, they store the keys necessary to access your crypto balance on the blockchain.

How Crypto Wallets Work

As we explained back in Chapter 2, a transaction consists of two addresses and the sum of coins being transferred between them. But what are these addresses exactly, and what do they have to do with your coins?

The first thing you must understand is that there are no actual bitcoins or altcoins anywhere. Coins of any cryptocurrency exist only as numbers within the blockchain. When you buy, sell, or use coins, the balance of your account is kept on the blockchain. Each balance is connected to a unique address that is generated by a cryptographic key that belongs to one user and one user only. This key is called the private key.

When you set up a crypto wallet, your wallet will contain a private key. This private key is a 52-character long alphanumeric string written in base-58. It is used to generate both the address of your balance and a public key. The public key allows you or anyone else who knows your public key to track your transactions and even your balance. However, no one but you knows your private key.

When you conduct a transaction, your private key is used to authenticate the transaction, but only your public key will be visible on the transaction itself. Your public key is essentially your digital signature. While you can generate your public key from your private key, you cannot go the other way around. This ensures that no one can figure out what your private key is.

Addresses are single-use numbers designed to be sent to someone when they are going to send you bitcoins. When a transaction is initiated, the receiver of the coins generates an address with their private key and sends it to the sender of the coins. The sender then uses that address to send the coins to the receiver. While addresses can be reused, it is recommended that a new address be generated for every transaction.

The See-Through Safe

Everything on the blockchain is transparent, including balances. That means someone could track someone else's transactions and balance history. But because addresses are written in a base-58 alphanumeric code that is 26 to 35 characters long and public keys are 130 character long hexadecimal numbers, you don't actually know what belongs to who. In essence, your balance is like a safe that everyone can see the contents of, but without your private key, no one can access your balance. This is what makes blockchain so secure. In order to access that balance, you need the private key associated with that balance in order to access it.

This makes your private key the most important piece of information you have when it comes to dealing with cryptocurrency, and your crypto wallet is what you use to store your private key or keys.

Hot Wallets

When dealing with crypto wallets, there are two types. The first type, hot wallets, also known as software wallets, are digital wallets that are used to store your key. These digital wallets allow you to quickly access your private key, letting you quickly carry out transactions. When buying, selling, or using crypto, hot wallets are generally preferred to help facilitate a fast transaction. There are three basic types of hot wallets to be aware of:

- **Desktop wallets** are apps that you install on your computer. These wallets are used to store your keys on your computer and validate any transactions you might make.

- Similar to desktop wallets, **mobile wallets** are crypto hot wallet apps you install on your phone. However, most mobile wallets do not store their information locally and are often just an interface for online wallets.

- **Online wallets** are wallets that are run on websites or services by a third party. Most exchanges have their own hot wallets where you can store the coins you buy and sell on the exchange.

While hot wallets can allow for quick and convenient access to your private key, they are not without risk.

Crypto Hacks and Thefts

If you've watched the news over the years, you will no doubt have heard stories now and then of hackers stealing bitcoins and other cryptocurrencies. As we discussed earlier, actually hacking the blockchain is next to impossible. Even a 51% attack will only affect new blocks that are generated by the attacker and not old blocks already added to the chain. It begs the question: How do hackers steal bitcoins? While crypto and the blockchain are quite secure, the systems that actually manage the coins are not always.

When hackers manage to steal bitcoins or other altcoins, what generally happens is the hackers gain access to a person's wallet and private key. They then use the private key to set up one or more transactions to send the coins associated with that key to the hacker's own balance. Due to the nature of the blockchain, once that transaction is completed, it cannot be undone. As far as the blockchain is concerned, those are no longer your coins.

While most hot wallets are secure, they are by no means impenetrable. The other issue with hot wallets is that the majority of them are managed not by the person who uses them. Rather, their data, including the private keys, are managed by the exchange or service that issues the hot wallet and stored on their servers. This means that if the service does not have adequate protection, a hacker can gain access to all the private keys they are storing and use them to drain you and everyone else's crypto balances dry.

Mt. Gox

One of the first and most well-known Bitcoin thefts was that of the Mt. Gox exchange. Originally launched in 2010, Mt. Gox, located in Shibuya Tokyo, Japan, quickly grew to one of the leading Bitcoin exchanges. By the start of 2014, Mt. Gox was handling over 70% of all Bitcoin transactions worldwide (Wikipedia, 2021). Things came to a halt however, on February 7th, 2014, when Mt. Gox stopped all Bitcoin withdrawals. By February 24th, Mt. Gox suspended all trading and shut down its website. That same day, a leak alleged that a hacker had stolen 744,408 bitcoins—most of which may have been stolen years before.

Mt. Gox would later confirm, while filing for bankruptcy protection, that it had lost approximately 750,000 of its customer's bitcoins and around 100,000 of its own bitcoins. This 850,000 coin total would later be amended to 650,000 bitcoins when 199,999.99 bitcoins were later found in an old crypto wallet that was used prior to June 2011, when the original hack was suspected to have occurred (Wikipedia Foundation, 2021t).

By April of 2015, authorities determined that most of the coins were stolen over several years, starting in late 2011, not long after a previous data breach in June of that year. While Alexander Vinnik, the owner of the Bitcoin exchange, BTC-e, would eventually be charged for laundering the stolen bitcoins, the coins themselves have yet to be recovered.

Cold Wallets

As we've shown, hot wallets are only as secure as the server or computer they are stored on. However, the other type of crypto wallets, cold wallets, are the exact opposite.

Cold wallets are devices, usually USB, that are designed to store your private key off the computer. When not being actively used, cold wallets are not connected to the Internet (assuming they can be).

Cold wallets tend to be far more secure than hot wallets mostly by virtue of the fact that they are not always online. Most hardware wallets will also have additional security protection on them in the form of PINs and other features to prevent them from being used if they are stolen. Hardware wallets are also designed to be difficult to hack when plugged in, providing some protection if the system they are plugged into should be compromised.

There are two types of cold wallets:

- **Hardware wallets** are devices, usually USB, that store your private keys. These wallets usually have to be plugged in to be used and often come with advanced security features like pin numbers or two-step authentication.

    o One of the two most well-known hardware wallet makers is **Ledger**. Ledger's wallets are currently some of the most popular hardware wallets on the market. Ledger wallets use a distinct operating system called BOLOS. Ledger also has its own software that you can install on your devices to allow for quickly accessing your stored wallets and keys. Ledger also uses a 24-word seed phrase to generate the wallet's private key. As long as you have this seed phrase, you can still retrieve your wallet's private key—even if you lose it.

o **Trezor** was the first legitimate and secure Bitcoin hardware wallet produced (Mitra, 2021). Unlike Ledger wallets that look more like small USB pen drives, Trezor wallets have a design similar to small calculators. Trezor wallets have a more isolated design that allows it to remain protected even if the system it is plugged into is compromised. The wallet's PIN and 24-word seed phrase are only entered into the wallet itself and never through an external device. Trezor hardware wallets, however, are more costly than other hardware wallets, including Ledger.

o Founded in 2019, **Prokey** is a newcomer to the hardware wallet industry and offers a unique multi-function wallet. Among its features is a web interface that allows you to access chromium-based web pages without the need to download potentially dangerous apps, extensions, or executable files. The wallet's firmware is also designed not to install anything that does not come from designated Prokey servers, adding another layer of protection to the device.

- **Paper wallets** are pieces of paper with your private key printed on them along with QR codes that can be scanned instead of having to manually type in the key when you use it. Paper wallets are perhaps the safest form of cold wallet, as they cannot be plugged into anything and therefore cannot be hacked. However, they are also made of paper and can be easily damaged, destroyed, or lost.

While cold wallets might be more secure than hot wallets, should they become damaged or stolen, you could potentially lose access to your private key. While some cold wallets have some form of retrieval method or service, it is best to keep your cold wallet in a secure and safe place when not in use in order to ensure that you will not need to use that service.

James Howells' Lost Fortune

Though this story does not involve a cold wallet, the story of James Howells' lost hard drive is one of the earliest examples in Bitcoin's history of what can happen if you misplace your cold wallet.

Back in 2009, James Howells, an IT engineer from Newport, Wales, began mining Bitcoin on his laptop. During his time as a Bitcoin miner, he amassed a total of 7,500 bitcoins. Eventually, he disassembled the laptop and sold it for parts but kept the hard drive with the private keys on it in case Bitcoin ever became valuable.

Fast forward to 2013. One day, while cleaning his house, Howells mistakenly throws out the hard drive containing his private keys. By the time he had realized the mistake, the garbage had been sent to the local landfill. Since then, Howells has been trying to recover the hard drive but has been, to this day, unsuccessful in trying to convince the Newport City Council to let him search and even dig up the landfill—an operation he himself would fund (Braddick, 2021).

Going by current prices, Howells' lost coins would be worth roughly a little more than $350 million. Unfortunately, unless he can retrieve his private keys, those coins are considered lost and will never be used ever again.

Howells' story is not unique. Hearing stories about people losing access to their funds because they have forgotten the passwords or PIN numbers to access their private keys, or lost their private keys/cold wallets, is not uncommon. They serve as a reminder that one must guard their cold wallet like they would guard any other precious item or asset, as failure to do so can have serious financial consequences (Braddick, 2021).

Which Wallet Should You Use?

The short answer to this question is both. The longer answer is that in order to buy, sell, or spend any crypto, you will need to put it in a hot wallet—that part is inescapable. However, the bulk of your coins should be stored in a separate cold wallet.

Hot wallets are intended mostly for carrying out transactions. However, if you are just looking to hold your coins for the foreseeable future, then you are better off putting them in a cold wallet and putting that cold wallet in a safe place until you are ready to use those coins.

How much of your coins you will keep in your hot wallet depends on how often you use it. If you plan to do some regular trading or spending, keeping a small amount of your coins in a hot wallet would be best. If you are only going to use your hot wallet to do trades every now and then, it would be better to keep all of your coins in a cold wallet, and only load some of your coins into your hot wallet when you need to. However, be aware that some exchanges might charge a transaction fee for moving your coins out of their hot wallet.

Ultimately, how you balance the use of your hot and cold wallets will be up to you. However, we do recommend you use a combination of both in order to keep your investment safe and secure.

Chapter 7:

Purchasing Bitcoin and Other

Cryptocurrencies

Now that you have your crypto wallets ready to fill with Bitcoin or other altcoins, it's time to actually purchase some coins.

Some Important Things to Know

The following are some important points to remember and consider when buying Bitcoin or any other cryptocurrency. These pieces of information will be key in helping you manage your crypto investment.

The Satoshi Unit

A dollar can be broken up into four quarters, 10 dimes, 20 nickels, or 100 pennies. While Bitcoin and other altcoins are not broken down along the same lines, they can be broken down.

Bitcoin and other altcoins can be broken down into units up to 100 millionth (0.00000001) of a coin. These units are called satoshi, named after Bitcoin's mysterious creator Satoshi Nakamoto. Bitcoin can also be broken down into units of 1,000 (0.001), called millibitcoin.

This division of Bitcoin and other altcoins is what allows people to purchase bitcoin, without spending the thousands needed to actually buy a complete coin. It should be noted, however, that it is only the coins with a very high price that are usually broken down this way. Stablecoins and other cryptos that have a low price point are generally sold in complete coin units or in smallest units.

The Crypto Market Never Sleeps

Unlike traditional markets that run on regular business hours, the crypto markets and exchanges never sleep. This means that the price of Bitcoin can change in the middle of the night or at the height of your day.

This has the advantage of letting a person manage their crypto investment at their own time and pace, rather than having to focus on it during a specific time frame. However, this can also mean that price crashes and rallies can go on at any time—even during the middle of the night while you are asleep.

When you begin investing, make sure to plan accordingly for this fact.

Make Sure You Hold Your Own Coins

Usually, when you purchase Bitcoin, the coins you purchase will be added to your balance. However, there are some instances where this does not happen. This is usually the case when you buy coins through an intermediary. Rather than the coins going to your wallet, they will go into the intermediary's wallet or a wallet you have with them.

This is not necessarily a bad thing. As we will go into more detail later on, there are some services where this does happen. However, outside of these specific cases, you want to have your coins deposited into your balance and wallet. The first step in keeping your coins secure is to get them into your possession and not someone else's. When your coins are held by someone else, you rely on their security—not your own. It also means that while that other entity is holding your coins, you might not be able to move them into your cold wallet should you choose to move them.

Crypto Exchanges

In order to safely purchase Bitcoin and other altcoins, you need to go through a crypto exchange. Similar to a stock exchange, crypto exchanges are where people go to buy and sell crypto, as well as monitor the price and even news about their crypto of choice.

Crypto exchanges are all online and can be accessed via a web browser. You will need to create an account on the exchange you want to use, and in most cases, register a hot wallet with the exchange.

As of the time of writing, there are 398 active exchanges. (Yes, in the time since writing Chapter 5, another exchange came online. This is not a mistake.) These are different exchanges around the world and not just in North America. Some of these exchanges are, to say the least, a little dubious. As such, before you commit to using a given exchange, take the time to do a little research on it to see if it is having or has had any issues.

Coinbase

Coinbase is currently the largest crypto exchange currently operating. Aside from Bitcoin, they also allow the trading of 50 other cryptos, including Ethereum and Dogecoin. Coinbase's interface is also simple to use and understand. Coinbase is also secure and does have some crypto insurance and FDIC insurance on cash balances. Coinbase can be accessed through either a desktop computer or via their mobile app on smartphones.

Coinbase also offers a number of tools and services, including recurring buys. However, most of these tools are only available with a free Coinbase Pro account. The standard Coinbase account also has higher fees then its pro counterpart. Also, like most exchanges, Coinbase controls the keys of your hot wallet. They do, however, offer a cold storage vault feature where you can store your coins offline. (We still recommend using your own cold wallet whenever possible). Coinbase also has more security than some other exchanges.

Overall, Coinbase is an excellent platform for people new to cryptocurrency and investing to learn about. Its simple interface allows one to learn about the process, while the pro accounts also introduce a number of other tools.

The Coinbase "Hack"

Just before the time of writing, stories began to circulate about a number of Coinbase clients who had their accounts hacked and drained. Based on the available information, it appears that hackers gained control of the client accounts through SIM swapping.

SIM swapping is a type of fraud where the fraudster takes control of the user's phone number. This is usually done by the fraudster gathering personal information on the user. Once the fraudster has sufficient information, they then contact the mobile provider and try to convince them to switch the phone number to a different SIM card. Once the fraudster has control of the phone number, they will receive all text and phone calls going to that number. SIM swapping allows the fraudster to bypass two-step authentication that rely on calling or texting the user's phone number. The fraudster receives all the calls and sent messages and is able to properly authenticate that they are the one trying to access the account.

As of the time of writing, all information concerning the Coinbase hack points to a number of victims falling prey to SIM swapping. If that indeed turns out to be the case, then technically, Coinbase itself hasn't been hacked, but various users on the platform have been. SIM swapping relies on the fraudster gaining enough personal information on the user; SIM swapping victims can also be victims of identity theft. Such thefts are carried out either by phishing emails and other means, including purchasing such information on the dark web or black market.

However, this is all based on information that was available at the time of writing. It is still too early to see how this event will ultimately affect Coinbase. Unless new information comes out that indicates otherwise, we still feel confident in recommending Coinbase for new investors wishing to start investing in crypto.

Regardless of how it plays out, this incident also shows the value of storing your unused coins offline in a cold wallet. Do not keep all of your coins in one wallet, and more importantly, do not keep all your coins online if you do not need to.

Binance and Binance.US

Binance is a very close second place to Coinbase's first place in terms of exchange popularity and size. However, where Coinbase is geared toward people who are new or have little experience with crypto and investing, Binance is the more advanced exchange for those who know what they are doing.

Binance is an international exchange, while Binance.US is an arm of the exchange geared specifically for the United States. However, Binance.US does not trade in as many altcoins as the main Binance site does, trading only 50+ different coins to Binance International's 300+. Binance.US is also not available in Connecticut, Hawaii, Idaho, Louisiana, New York, Texas, and Vermont.

Aside from low fees, Binance has a plethora of tools available to advanced users, including different trading order types and two powerful trading dashboards of data (Tepper & Schmidt, 2021). Both Binance sites also allow the staking of some cryptos.

If you plan on doing serious crypto trading and are versed in the nuances of finance and investment, then either Binance site would be better suited for you. However, if you want to focus on trading more in altcoins, the Binance international website would be the better choice for you.

Binance Coin (BNB)

The Binance exchange has its own crypto: Binance Coin. Originally, Binance Coin ran off of Ethereum's blockchain, but as the exchange grew in size and popularity, Binance created its own blockchain and coin.

Binance Coin was used as a utility token for trading fees that were discontinued in 2017 (Frankenfield, 2021c). Since then, the coin has evolved to be used in a number of ways both on and off the Binance exchange. On the exchange, if you pay for Binance's services and fees with Binance Coin, you will receive a discount. You can also use Binance Coin to book travel accommodations; make credit card payments; make loans or transfers; and even make donations. However, most of these services are linked indirectly to Binance itself via its international website. Outside of the Binance ecosystem, Binance Coin is not as widely accepted.

Currently, Binance coin is worth around $470. If you do not plan on doing much trading on the Binance exchange, then it's not recommended that you acquire this altcoin. However, if you plan to make the Binance Exchange your home, then we recommend you invest in some of this crypto to use to pay for services on the exchange instead of with fiat.

Kraken

Founded in 2011, Kraken is one of the oldest U.S. crypto exchanges currently active. Like Coinbase, it has a high cybersecurity rating and has a host of tools and features for both newcomers and experienced crypto traders. They also have low fees and allow for the staking of some altcoins.

Though not a powerhouse like Coinbase or Binance, Kraken is still a noteworthy exchange we would recommend.

PayPal

First off, PayPal is not a true exchange compared to other exchanges we have listed so far. PayPal only allows for the purchase of four types of crypto on its platform: Bitcoin, Ethereum, Litecoin, and Bitcoin Cash. Like exchanges, PayPal manages your private keys, but unlike exchanges, you cannot currently remove your coins from your PayPal wallet. PayPal also lets you pay for purchases through its service using your crypto when available.

The main concern with PayPal is that any crypto you purchase through the company is not yours. Rather, PayPal buys the crypto on your behalf, holds in on your behalf, and spends or sells it on your behalf. You cannot transfer any crypto you buy through PayPal outside of PayPal—not even to a cold wallet.

This makes PayPal a sort of pseudo-exchange and allows for a more hands-off approach to investing in crypto. However, the inability to withdraw your coins is perhaps the biggest drawback of the service. Though PayPal is seen as being a very safe and secure service, only time will tell if the crypto part of the service will be as secure.

If you want to invest in crypto but do not want the hassle of dealing with some of its aspects, like crypto wallets, PayPal would be the way to go. However, if you are serious about investing in Bitcoin or altcoins, we still recommend using a proper crypto exchange.

Chapter 8:

Other Ways to Invest in Bitcoin

Actually buying Bitcoin or altcoins is not the only way to invest in cryptocurrency. There are other more traditional routes one can consider if they wish for a slightly less volatile alternative.

Staking

Before we get into ways to invest in cryptocurrency without actually buying coins, there is one method of investing in crypto that is quite stable and can give you more regular rewards. That is staking.

As mentioned previously, proof-of-stake is a new way of crypto mining that is less resource intensive and more environmentally friendly than the proof-of-work model used by most cryptos, including Bitcoin. Holders of coins stake a part of their coins to be used in the mining process and receive a reward in the form of network fees. These fees are usually in the form of more network coins, which can be used or traded. Unlike proof-of-work, which is a race to find the next hash number first, proof-of-stake is fairer, and anyone who stakes coins will get some form of reward for their stake.

Proof-of-stake is still in its infancy, so it will still be some time before we determine if the system will truly work as intended.

However, that has not stopped a number of altcoins, including Ethereum 2.0 and Cardano, from adopting proof-of-stake as opposed to proof of work.

Both the Binance and Kraken exchanges offer staking opportunities. However, of the two, Kraken offers more staking opportunities. Staking is also not a short-term commitment. The longer you stake your coins, the more you will get in return.

Since staking is mostly done with newer altcoins, these coins do not generally have the greatest of value. Of the coins available on Kraken, for example, Ethereum 2.0 is the highest value coin available to stake. However, Kraken also offers several off-chain staking opportunities for Bitcoin (BTC), the euro (EUR), and the U.S. dollar (USD).

If one does choose to try staking, we recommend only staking altcoins that are confirmed to be using the proof-of-stake method. Any staking that involves proof-of-work coins like bitcoins are doing something different from the proof-of-stake method. While such off-chain staking is not always fraudulent in nature, they should be thoroughly researched before you decide to stake your cash or coins in them.

Crypto Savings Accounts

Similar to staking, crypto savings accounts are special savings accounts where you can store your crypto and earn interest on your coins. Unlike regular savings accounts, crypto savings accounts have a much higher interest rate. The leading savings account, BlockFi, for example, offers up to 8.6% Interest rates on your investment (Horvath, 2021).

However, while such high interest rates might be appealing, they do not come without risk. These crypto savings accounts are, for the most part, not insured. You also lose control of any of the coins that are sent to a savings account while they are there, and while the company has your coins, you do not necessarily know what they are doing with them. Also, you may be limited in when and how much of your coins you can withdraw from the savings account at a given time, though this will vary between providers.

While it's not advised against using crypto savings accounts, they're not really recommended either. Staking is the safer option, particularly when done from either a trusted exchange or service. If you do wish to make use of a crypto savings account, make sure you do your due diligence and are fully aware of how the account will work.

Crypto-Related Stocks

One of the simplest ways to indirectly invest in the cryptocurrency boom is to invest in stocks related to it. Recently, a number of major companies have turned their attention to the cryptocurrency market and are either buying into the market by acquiring bitcoins and other altcoins or are looking to expand their services into it. Others have benefitted from the cryptocurrency hype indirectly.

The other benefit of crypto-related stocks is that you are not betting on any one crypto directly nor are you subjecting yourself to crypto's volatility. While the company owning the stocks might be, you are betting instead on the company rather than the coins they are investing in. Of course, the stock market is a stable place, more than the crypto market, so it's something some see as a much safer bet. Here are a few stocks worth considering:

- **NVIDIA** and **Advanced Micro Devices (AMD)** are the two biggest makers of computer graphics cards and GPUs. Both companies have seen their sales surge in part thanks to the crypto mining boom. While the largest mining operations have since moved onto ASIC-based rigs, part-time miners and crypto-enthusiasts still rely on GPUs as their primary processor of choice for mining altcoins. The demand is still high enough that NVIDIA has developed a dedicated mining GPU for Ethereum and other altcoins. Even if NVIDIA's CMP HX GPU does not do well, miners will still be buying their other GPU offerings.

- A traditional computer company, **IBM** is leveraging the power of the private blockchain to provide next generation solutions for supply chains. They have already seen success with several companies, including Kroger and True Tickets, and have the potential to see explosive growth with their blockchain technology sector in the coming years.

- As we have already shown in previous chapters, **PayPal** has been investing significant amounts into their foray into the crypto currency market.

- **Mastercard** is stepping into cryptocurrency and blockchain with recent partnerships. They are working with blockchain technology company R3 to develop a new blockchain-based cross-border payment system that, if successful, would give them a major advantage in sending money internationally. They are also working with the Gemini cryptocurrency exchange to develop a cash-back card on up to 30 different cryptocurrencies that will be supported by the card.

- **CME GROUP**, the world's largest futures and options exchange, is currently the only exchange that offers a market for Bitcoin futures contracts. As interest in crypto continues to rise, CME is looking to increase its participation in the cryptocurrency market.

- As we talked about in the previous chapter, **Coinbase** is currently the top crypto exchange currently operating. It is also a publicly traded company that debuted on the stock market in April of 2021 and is one of the best crypto-related stocks available.

These are of course just a few of the companies that have an invested interest in cryptocurrency and the blockchain. There are many other companies that are turning their attention to Bitcoin and other cryptos that would make excellent stocks for you to purchase.

Blockchain-Related ETFs

If one does not want to take the time to pick and choose which individual companies to invest in, another alternative would be to invest in a blockchain or crypto-focused Exchange-Traded Fund (ETF). ETFs are a hybrid fund that is part stock and part fund. Unlike regular mutual funds, ETFs are traded regularly throughout the day like stocks. Also, unlike regular stocks which are generally for individual companies, an ETF can hold any number and combination of stocks. ETFs can also contain bonds and even assets.

One way to look at ETFs is that they are large, diverse portfolios managed by others that you can buy shares in. They are secure and stable, and like stocks, they are less risky to trade in than crypto coins.

Currently, there are three Blockchain ETFs trading in the United States.

All values and information listed in this section were taken at the time of writing and are subject to change.

- **Amplify Transformational Data Sharing ETF (BLOK)** is currently ranked first place of the three ETFs we will discuss. This actively managed ETF has at least 80% of its net assets invested in blockchain-related companies. Currently BLOK's net assets have a total value of $1,246,514,858, and its top three stocks include Microstrategy Inc, Hut 8 Mining Group, and Marathon Digital (Amplify ETFs, 2020).

- **The Siren Nasdaq NexGen Economy ETF (BLCN)** follows the Nasdaq Blockchain Economy Index (RSBLCN), which focuses on companies and stocks invested in blockchain. The ETF contains a mix of value stocks and growth stocks from companies that perform well on the index. Currently, BLNC's net assets have a total value of $125,954,167, and its top three holdings are Huobi Technology Holdings,

Coinbase Global Inc., and Square Inc. (SirenETFs, 2020).

- **First Trust Indxx Innovative Transaction & Process ETF (LEGR)** is the final ETF on our list. It follows the Indxx Blockchain Index and invests at least 90% of its net asset on stocks and depository receipts that feature on the index. Currently, LEGR's net assets have a total value of $125,954,167, and its top holdings are NVIDIA Corporation, Advanced Micro Devices, Inc. (AMD), and WIPRO Limited (APR) (First Trust Portfolios L.P., 2021).

- An honorable mention is the **Bitwise Crypto Industry Innovators ETF (BITQ)**. BITQ only recently launched in May of 2021. Since it's new, there is not enough data to yet determine how well this ETF will do. Currently, BITQ's net assets have a total value of $71,863,685, and its top three holdings are Microstrategy, Coinbase Global Inc, and Silvergate Capital.

Chapter 9:

Bitcoin vs. Fiat Currency and

Precious Metals

Since its creation, Bitcoin has been declared dead or dying approximately 427 times, including 34 times so far in 2021 (99 Bitcoins, 2021). While I have no doubt there are many people in the world who would like to see Bitcoin and cryptocurrencies in general die off, the fact of the matter is that crypto is here to stay. However, we have to see how cryptos like Bitcoin and Ethereum are ultimately going to fit into the world economy.

As we have shown so far in this book, cryptos and the underlying blockchain have great potential to revolutionize a number of aspects when it comes to digital commerce and beyond. However, as they are, cryptos are not going to find their place in the global economy anytime soon.

Bitcoin vs. Fiat Currency

Contrary to what some crypto enthusiasts might hope, Bitcoin—or any other crypto for that matter—is never going to replace the fiat currency of a nation. The fact is governments require a stable currency that they can use to help manage their economy. Central banks, in order to help keep economies running smoothly, will print money or take money out of circulation in order to keep their currency strong and fight off inflation.

The public blockchains cryptocurrencies run on are essentially trustless: No one node or entity on the network is trusted any more than the other. While this trustless environment is good for keeping anyone from meddling with the currency or the underlying blockchain, it is the primary reason why governments will, have been, and in some cases, continue to avoid Bitcoin and the other altcoins.

A government's fiscal policy relies in large part on the stability of its fiat currency. This stability allows them to forecast and plan ahead for when times are good and when times go bad. While this has shown to not always be the case in practice, imagine the trouble a government would have if their fiat currency had the same volatility as Bitcoin.

While pegging a fiat currency to a crypto would help stabilize its price, a government could manipulate the price of the crypto by manipulating its fiat currency. This is not just a potentially dangerous practice, but it also goes against the original idea of bitcoin as being a decentralized digital currency. More importantly, crypto communities would not take this sort of meddling lightly. The only way to avoid this problem would be to return to something similar to the gold standard when pegging a crypto, where the value of a government's fiat would be based on the amount of gold they currently hold.

Control is the second issue governments face with crypto. In order for any changes to the network to be made, a near total majority of consensus must be reached within the community.

Failure to do so can result in splits within the community, which in turn can result in a hard forking of the blockchain. Forking of this nature would undermine confidence in the crypto and its community and could have other adverse effects besides the results of the forking itself.

As we have seen in the politics of some Western nations of late, trying to get a near total majority of people to agree on anything can be quite difficult. Imagine if a government needed to quickly implement a change to a public blockchain in order to avert a financial crisis. How long would it take to get a consensus? What if there was a strong opposition to the change? If a government was met with genuine opposition in order to get the change through, bedlam would ensue.

The third issue crypto has is scalability. As we've already explained, the proof-of-work model of crypto mining is inefficient and does not scale well when the network is hit with high volumes of traffic. Bitcoin alone takes an average of 10 minutes to mine a block, and its transaction times are not very competitive.

For example, as we showed earlier, the average time to complete a Bitcoin transaction on August 30th, 2021, was 14.73 minutes (YCharts, 2021). Compare that to Visa, which carries out approximately 1,700 transactions a second (Mainfinex, 2021). Bitcoin's performance was also during a day of relatively light traffic on Bitcoin's network. On July 3rd, 2021, Bitcoin's network suffered such heavy congestion that the average transaction time reached a peak of 634.80 minutes (YCharts, 2021). This is not even the highest peak so far in 2021 either.

As you can see, Bitcoin's performance compared to Visa is abysmal. While there are other altcoins that have faster transaction times, few are capable of matching the bar set by

Visa. The first was EOS, which was launched in 2018, and this is a bar that must be met or exceeded for any crypto that could be considered for use by a government.

Finally, perhaps the biggest issue cryptos have is regulation. Though various governments around the world have been making headway within their jurisdictions, the cryptocurrency market remains, for the most part, unregulated. Any crypto that is adopted by a government is going to have to be fairly regulated—something many crypto enthusiasts will not be pleased with.

Needless to say, the case against a government adopting crypto is fairly strong, but that does not mean that governments cannot make use of crypto and the blockchain.

Rather than adopting a cryptocurrency for their own use, governments will most likely follow China's lead and tokenize their fiat currency with a private blockchain, creating a digital version of their currency. This will allow a government to control their blockchain and crypto, while at the same time allowing them to compete with other cryptos on public blockchains.

That is not to say that there is no room for cryptocurrencies. It's ultimately still too early to tell what the future holds for crypto. Based on the investments being made into Bitcoin and other altcoins, it's only a matter of time before they become another common payment method as debit eventually did after it was first introduced.

Bitcoin vs. Gold

Prior to 1933, the U.S. government followed the gold standard as a means of placing value on their currency. The gold standard set a fixed price for gold that governments would buy and sell at. They would then use that fixed price to determine the value of their currency. The gold standard was first introduced in the 1870 and was eventually moved away from in 1933, though the United States would not be completely free of the gold standard until much later in 1971.

Since gold was first discovered, humanity has had a love affair with the yellow metal. Even after the gold standard was abolished, investors still flock to gold when the market sees a downturn. Though it does not have a place in dictating money policy anymore, gold is still seen as a safe-haven asset—a place where one can store wealth during difficult times and later sell it to recoup the investment or, more often than not, at a profit.

Gold is not just a safe-haven asset either. Besides the inherent desire for gold, the yellow metal is also very malleable, making it ideal for use in the design and construction of jewelry, including gold teeth. Gold is also a highly effective conductor and is used in many electronics, including smartphones and computers. It is even used in the construction of shuttles and other space vehicles and devices like satellites.

However, recently, and particularly during the pandemic, gold is being challenged as the top safe-haven asset by Bitcoin.

Though not a physical coin, Bitcoin shares some investment-type properties with gold. Both Bitcoin's price and gold's price tends to move inversely with the dollar. This means that when the value of the dollar drops, their price rises. Despite the crashes in price Bitcoin has endured, it has so far not only recovered from but still continues to rise in value.

Aside from these similarities, Bitcoin has several advantages over gold. The first is its security. It's easier to make fake gold or commit fraud with gold, than it is with Bitcoin. Thanks to the blockchain, Bitcoin cannot be forged or altered. Since it's a digital currency, Bitcoin is also much easier to store and transport than gold. A single gold bar's value pales in comparison to the value of a single Bitcoin, and it can be stored in a hardware wallet as small as a USB pen drive or on a piece of paper. As we've already shown, anyone can buy Bitcoin or altcoins. Gold, on the other hand, is not always so easily acquired.

However, Bitcoin is still not an accepted form of currency or legal tender across the world. Bitcoin's volatile price makes it potentially hazardous as a safe-haven asset. Gold, on the other hand, is universally accepted and, more importantly, regulated. Its price is stable and not prone to the same epic rises and falls that Bitcoin is. In terms of financial investment, despite the difference in price, gold is still considered the safer investment for the time being.

During the COVID-19 pandemic, gold's price has remained stable for the most part, but Bitcoin has continued to reach new heights. However, Bitcoin has also seen a crash in April of this year that wiped out almost half of its value. While it has since recovered and is still on the rise, such crashes are bound to happen again.

While Bitcoin is a strong competitor against gold, it's too early to say if it will ultimately replace gold as a safe-haven asset. Though not as valuable currently as compared to Bitcoin, gold has a much longer history and has proven stability against economic downturns and chaos that Bitcoin does not yet have.

Will Bitcoin Still Be King?

Another thing to consider is that while Bitcoin may be the first and still most popular crypto, that may not always be so. Compared to other cryptocurrencies, Bitcoin has a number of flaws, including its scalability and inefficient proof-of-work. It also has a somewhat checkered history when it comes to its involvement in crime. While most of these issues could be resolved in the future, it would require the Bitcoin community to enact changes across the Bitcoin network that many of its members may not be interested in.

Ethereum, the consistently second place altcoin to Bitcoin's first place, is not just a crypto but also an entire development platform complete with tools that developers can use to build dApps and even entire decentralized financial programs. Ethereum was also the one to introduce smart contracts—a powerful tool that has been adopted not only by other cryptos, including Bitcoin, but also by private blockchain users and developers. Its 2.0 update will also move Ethereum from proof-of-work to proof-of-stake—a much more efficient and environmentally friendly process for mining blocks.

Still waiting in the wings is Cardano, a third-generation crypto that was made to overcome Ethereum's deficiencies and ultimately replace it. Whether it will become more popular than Ethereum remains to be seen, but it is a strong competitor that cannot be overlooked.

In terms of dependability, altcoins like Bitcoin Cash and Litecoin have improved their mining and overall performance to process transactions much faster than Bitcoin. Though nowhere near as popular as Bitcoin, they make better alternatives to Bitcoin as a spending currency, and more altcoins are becoming as efficient.

Aside from being the first cryptocurrency, Bitcoin still has the world's attention—the driving force behind its growth and popularity. However, much of that attention is based on hype. Behind the scenes, where the real work is going on, the blockchain technology is slowly gaining traction and revolutionizing the way we use and store data. While they do not have as many big names attached to them, Ethereum, Cardano, and a few other altcoins are slowly gaining serious investment and consideration.

Whether Bitcoin will be able to live up to the hype that surrounds it remains to be seen. Certainly, if it ever should lose its popularity, other altcoins are ready to pounce on the opportunity to replace Bitcoin as the top crypto in the world. While it is still possible for Bitcoin to evolve and fix its current deficiencies, that will hinge almost entirely on the willingness of the Bitcoin community to evolve.

However, for the time being, that is not a question they need to overly concern themselves with. Bitcoin is still going strong, and for now, it shows no sign of slowing down.

Chapter 10:

Putting an Exit Strategy

Together

It's fitting that in the final chapter of this book, we talk about getting out of the cryptocurrency market. This does not necessarily mean a permanent exit, mind you. So far, we have talked about getting into the crypto market either by buying coins directly or indirectly through stocks and ETFs. But when dealing with the crypto market directly, one needs to know when to bow out in order to keep whatever profit they've made or risk suffering a loss. Crypto's volatility makes the odds of suffering such a loss more likely.

Bitcoin and Taxes

Though not a legal tender outside of El Salvador, Bitcoin and other altcoins are considered by most jurisdictions to be assets. This means that they can, and most assuredly are, taxed. In the United States, the IRS is being even more aggressive in cracking down on crypto tax compliance. Whether you are a small-time investor dabbling in crypto for the first time or a seasoned crypto trader, if you do not report your crypto earnings on your taxes, you could find yourself standing rather uncomfortably before the taxman.

Trying to go through all the details on taxes and crypto would be a book in itself. However, here are a few points to remember:

- For tax purposes, cryptocurrency of any kind, Bitcoin, or altcoins are considered property. This means that similar to stocks, bonds, and real estate, they are subject to capital gains and losses.

- If you earn crypto through mining, staking, interest, or even as a salary from employment, it is treated as income and therefore subject to income tax based on the value of those earnings in USD.

- Selling, trading, or spending (disposing) of crypto are taxable events that are subject to capital gains and losses. Buying and holding crypto—or moving crypto from a wallet you own to another wallet you own—are not taxable events.

Navigating the tax system of any country can be daunting. Do not be afraid to seek help in the form of a professional accountant if necessary. There are also a number of online tools and software that can also help you prepare your crypto-related tax forms. Here is a sample of three for your consideration:

- **CryptoTrader.tax** is an online service that lets you download your trading history from a number of crypto exchanges and compiles them into a report you can download and use to help file your taxes. It also generates pre-filled tax forms based on your data, including IRS Form 8949, which is a necessary form for crypto-related tax filings. CryptoTrader.tax is also partnered with TurboTax, allowing you to integrate the report into a TurboTax or TaxAct filing. Using CryptoTrader.tax's service is free, but you must pay a fee to generate and download the report—including any associated files.

- **TokenTax** is a more complete tax software with a larger suite of tools. It also supports most crypto exchanges, can generate tax forms including IRS Form 8949, and can be used in most jurisdictions around the world. Like CryptoTrader.tax, it can integrate with TurboTax and is also backed by a full team of accountants. However, it is more expensive than some of the other options available, and the basic version only has access to three exchanges. Overall, TokenTax is ideally suited to more experienced crypto traders with larger numbers of transactions to process.

- Focused more on defi application support, **ZenLedger** is considered one of the better crypto tax software for beginners. It has the same exchange support and TurboTax integration as the other two we've mentioned so far and also generates tax forms, including IRS Form 8949. However, some of its better support features and DeFi functions are only available in the paid versions of the software. It also only supports U.S. tax forms, so is not ideal for other parts of the world.

There are of course many more offerings than these available. Whichever you end up using, make sure you do your due diligence before committing to your final choice in order to make sure that it is the right one for you.

Formulating an Exit Strategy

As we mentioned at the start of this chapter, creating an exit strategy does not mean permanently leaving the cryptocurrency market. The idea behind an exit strategy is to manage your investment to maximize your gains and minimize your losses. This is particularly necessary when dealing with something as volatile as the cryptocurrency market.

An exit strategy will also help to make sure you understand what you are getting into. Anyone can enter the cryptocurrency market, but if you do not know what you are doing, you risk losing much or all of your investment. Having a plan going in will help to mitigate the risk of loss and ensure that you profit from your investment.

Before we go into more detail on exit strategies, here are some other things you will need to consider.

Start Small

If you are new to investing, one of the most important lessons we cannot stress enough is to start small. Do not invest money you cannot afford to lose. While this bit of advice can hold true for any form of investment, crypto's more volatile markets make this a much more mandatory piece of advice. Volatility aside, your crypto investment is also more prone to being stolen by bad actors like scammers and hackers.

One does not have to go far to find stories of people who have lost large amounts of money not just to the crypto markets but also to scams and hacks. Once you lose that money, the odds of recouping the loss are incredibly low. Coins in particular, Bitcoin or otherwise, once lost are highly unlikely to be recovered. That is why most financial experts only advise investing no more than 10% of your portfolio in crypto.

Do Not Get Greedy

Another piece of advice that is particularly relevant to the crypto market is to not be greedy. Despite the gains bitcoins and other altcoins have made, crypto is still considered a high-risk investment. As profitable as Bitcoin has been, it has also seen equal losses.

Unless you plan to hunker down for the long run, do not try and predict or play the market unless you are well-versed in doing so. Even then, crypto's volatility still has the potential to catch you by surprise.

When you formulate your exit strategy, set goals that are realistic. The profit you gain from your current investment will help fuel larger gains in your next venture. If you are trying to earn money for something, like the purchase of a new car, aim to stay comfortably within that goal. Do not overreach if you can help it; otherwise, you risk losing it all.

Do Not Get Caught up in the FOMO

Investing in crypto is not for the faint of heart. One of the real issues with the cryptocurrency market is FOMO: the fear of missing out.

Crypto's volatility can cause change in many ways: sometimes for the worse but other times for the better. Swings in the price of Bitcoin and other altcoins can open up opportunities investors can pounce on. However, sometimes, those opportunities can do more harm than good, particularly if it forces you to step outside of your currently set bounds and strategies. If you are not careful, such missteps could cause you to suffer more losses in the long run than originally anticipated.

Unless you are the type of person who thrives on gambling and chaos, stick to your plan. If that opportunity does not fit into your plan and exit strategy, not to mention the limit of the amount of money you can invest, stay the course and ignore it.

Do Not Be Afraid to Bow Out Early

Investing in crypto is not for the weak of heart. The crypto market's volatility makes it a much more stressful investment compared to the more traditional stock market. All it takes is one story, or even just one tweet, to send the price of Bitcoin rising or crashing. Often, you won't know when that will happen. Investing in the crypto market is in some ways like gambling: There is an element of luck and partial chaos to it that makes it difficult to accurately predict.

Due to this, it's unsurprising that most investment experts would advise you to not risk your money in crypto. Of course, it's never been the intention to dissuade you from investing in crypto. However, if you should decide to invest in crypto, you must be prepared for failure as well as success. One way or another, "a fool and his money are soon parted." Do not be that fool.

If you do invest into the crypto market and feel like it is more than you can handle, do not be afraid to exit before you've met your goals. If you no longer have confidence in your strategy or things are starting to go wrong, do not be afraid to cut your losses and exit earlier than planned. It's better to only lose part of your investment than most or all of it.

Sample Exit Strategies

Each crypto exchange will have different tools and options available to you to help you manage your investment. Rather than try and go through all the individual tools, we will instead focus on two strategies that you can use.

The goal of an exit strategy is to sell your coins for fiat currency at a total net gain. Again, how you set up your exit strategy will depend on the exchange you use and the tools they make available to you.

When you set your goals, try to ensure that you at least achieve breakeven. Try to earn a profit close or equal to the amount of your initial investment. In this way, even if you are not successful in seeing a profit, you will have at least mitigated the loss by recouping most or all of your initial investment.

Also, plan to reinvest your profits. Unless you are aiming to reach a specific goal, to truly maximize your profit potential, you will have to invest it multiple times. With each cycle of investment, assuming that you do not suffer a net loss, you will be able to invest more of your profit, resulting in even more profit. However, always make sure to set aside some of that profit in order to make sure you do not lose it all.

Buying and Selling at Predetermined Points

The first and easiest exit strategy is to pick a price point or percentage of growth in your coin of choice and sell your coins when the coin reaches that number. Likewise, setting a similar price point for when your coin's price dips to buy coins can be just as useful. Most exchanges offer tools to let buy and sell either recurrently on a fixed time frame or based on predetermined conditions. You can also do this manually by setting a minimum buy and sell price based on the amount of money you wish to invest and making purchases and sales when those points are reached.

The price at which you buy and sell at will be determined in part by the current price of the coin you wish to invest in and its recent trajectories. The old adage, "buy low, sell high" can apply here, but do not wait too long for the price of your coin to go the way you want it to. Remember that the crypto market is a volatile market, and once it starts going in one direction or the other, it will very likely not stop exactly where needed.

A Two-Step Exit

One way of exiting the crypto market is to do so in two steps. The idea behind this method is to ensure that you recoup your initial investment before you see any actual profit. This allows you to reach a break-even point should things go horribly wrong.

After making your initial investment in coins, divide the coins into two groups. Group A will be sold early on, as soon as the price reaches a point where the total net gain will equal your initial investment expenditure. This way, any gains made from Group B will be pure profit.

The size of your groupings will be determined by the value of the coins and the rate at which their value increases. If your coin's price is rising quickly, your Group A might be smaller than your group B, as you will need fewer coins to achieve a break-even point. However, if the price of your coins is lower or the price suffers a crash, the amount of coins in your Group A might be equal to or larger than your Group B.

This two-step method can be a little more difficult to manage rather than keeping your coins in a single pile, but this will ensure that your current investment does not end up losing you money.

Incremental Selling

Another, more advanced exit strategy is your coins incrementally. This method is useful if you are looking to try and maximize your profits but requires a little more work and possibly the use of automated trading tools.

The idea behind incremental selling is to sell certain amounts of coins at certain price points rather than selling all your coins at the same time. For example, when the price reaches 5% above your original purchase price, you would sell 10% of your coins. When it reaches 10%, you would sell another 10%. When the price gets much higher, say, 20% or 25%, you would sell 20% of your coins, and so on. You keep going until you've either sold all of your coins (If you are looking for a complete exit), or until you have 5% to 10% remaining.

This method will better allow you to slowly divest yourself of your coins and will bring in profit more consistently. While it may not potentially bring in as much as selling all your coins might at the highest price, this method will help keep you from getting too greedy. What's more, if your exchange has the necessary tools, you could automate these sales when they reach the desired price points.

As for which prices to sell at, that will be determined by which coin you chose to invest in and how well their prices are currently rising. You could use an incremental scale up to 10% for smaller value coins or jump as big as $10,000, $25,000, or even $50,0000 with more valuable coins like Bitcoin. An incremental exit is also a more long-term strategy depending on how fast your coin grows in value.

Time: Friend or Enemy?

Regardless of whether you chose either of these strategies or some other strategy, the next question you must ask yourself is this: How long are you willing to wait?

Most normal investments will increase in value over time, either becoming more valuable or receiving interest on the investment. While crypto has been shown to become more valuable over time, it's also shown that it is prone to sometimes horrific price crashes. Since there is no way to accurately predict when these crashes will happen, the longer you wait, the more likely there is to be another crash. Time, in this case, is a double-edged sword that will cut you if you are not careful.

When formulating your plan and exit strategy, you must determine how long you plan on going on before selling your coins. This is a bit of a loaded question though, as there are many factors to consider: How fast is the value of the coin growing? What is the current outlook of the coin? Do experts think it will continue to grow in the near future, or is it due for a crash? Is there some event about to happen in the near future that could affect the price of your coins? How much profit are you looking to gain? Do you have a time limit before you must pull out regardless of the outcome?

Regular investors will tend to look at the mid to long game, while short-term investors like day traders will try and turn their coins around on a daily basis. Whichever way you wish to go, make sure you have an idea of how long you want to keep your coins before selling them. Once you have this time frame in mind, you'll be better able to determine at what price points you want to sell at.

Spending Your Coins

While it will perhaps not make you a profit, spending your crypto is also another viable exit strategy. Bitcoin was designed to be a digital currency that was made to be spent, and if you should choose to spend it, there are options available.

Currently, there are more than 15,000 businesses worldwide that accept Bitcoin and some other altcoins (Jacquelyn, 2021). In 2020, a survey conducted by HSB shows that 36% of businesses in the U.S. accept bitcoin (Beigel, 2021). Most businesses that accept Bitcoin also accept some altcoins, including Ethereum, Litecoin, and Bitcoin Cash, to name a few. A rare few also accept Dogecoin, though again, this isn't recommended to acquire. Here is a list of places where you can spend your bitcoins and altcoins at:

- **Microsoft**, **Home Depot**, and **Starbucks** are a few of the big name brands that accept Bitcoin. **Xbox** also accepts Bitcoin through Microsoft.

- Movie theater company **AMC** will accept Bitcoin as payment for movie tickets across its U.S. theaters by the end of 2021.

- **Tesla** was to accept Bitcoin as payment for its vehicles for a short time but has put Bitcoin transactions on hold until more than 50% of mining is done with renewable energy (Walsh, 2021).

- Online websites **Overstock**, **Newegg**, and **Shopify** are a few that accept Bitcoin and other cryptos as payment.

- **Purse.io** is a website that lets you indirectly shop on Amazon and pay for your purchases with Bitcoin.

- The NHL team **San Jose Sharks** accept Bitcoin, Ethereum and Dogecoin for the purchase of season tickets and suite leases. The NBA Team **Dallas Mavericks** also accept the same three coins for the purchase of tickets and merchandise. Both accept crypto through BitPay.

- **Gyft** is a website that allows you to purchase gift cards with bitcoin from hundreds of retailers, including Best Buy, Amazon, Home Depot, and GameStop.

- Travel website **Bitcoin.Travel** allows you to book travel accommodations with Bitcoin. Travel website, **Expedia**, also accepts Bitcoin as payment when booking hotel rooms.

- Search engines like **Spendabit** and **BitcoinWide.com** will help you find businesses that accept Bitcoin.

- As we mentioned back in Chapter 7, **PayPal** allows you to checkout with Bitcoin, Ethereum, Litecoin or Bitcoin Cash through their service when applicable. However, this can only be done with coins purchased through PayPal.

Conclusion

Cryptocurrency and the blockchain's greatest chapters are yet to be written. Though a little over a decade old, we have yet to see the full potential of the blockchain, while Bitcoin and the other altcoins have yet to find their proper place in the global economy. It's difficult to say when we will reach those lofty peaks, but one thing is for certain: Bitcoin isn't going away anytime soon.

With the information you have gleaned from within the pages of this book, you are now ready to begin investing in cryptocurrency. And if our book has dissuaded you from investing in crypto, then we at least hope it was an informative and interesting read. Regardless of what your next endeavor may be, we wish you nothing but the best of luck in it.

Before we part ways, let us review some key points of this book.

1. Bitcoin and Altcoins Are Very Secure but Not Always the Networks That Manage Them.

The blockchain by its very design is made to be almost impossible to hack without gaining at least 51% control over its total network. Even then, you still cannot alter the blocks that have come before. However, while this makes crypto and the blockchain highly secure, the exchanges and services that manage crypto are not always so. The weakest link in the crypto network is your wallet and the system that manages it.

2. Crypto Runs on Public Blockchains.

Public blockchains are run by a community of individuals that anyone can join. This creates a trustless environment that ensures no one person or entity can manipulate the network and the crypto associated with that network. This includes governments, financial institutes, and big businesses. In order for changes to be made to the crypto or the software running the blockchain, the majority of the network has to agree. Otherwise, issues can occur which can split the blockchain and the network.

3. Private Blockchains Have the Potential to Shake Up the Way We Do Business.

Business-run private blockchains have great potential to change the way we manage data, supply chains, banking, and even voting. They offer a way to store and manage data in an incredibly secure environment that was not previously possible. We are only just now beginning to see the potential of what can be accomplished with the blockchain and are still many years away from achieving its full potential.

4. Crypto Is Volatile, and That Won't Change Anytime Soon.

Since Bitcoin and most altcoins are not pegged to any fiat currency or asset and currently do not have the backing of any legitimate government or financial institute, their price is purely speculative and can rise or fall on a whim. While we do not doubt that Bitcoin's popularity will continue to cause it and other altcoin prices to rise, they will also be prone to crashing as well.

5. Bitcoin Might Replace Gold, but It Won't Replace Fiat.

While it is possible Bitcoin might replace gold as a safe haven asset at some point in the future, neither Bitcoin nor any other altcoin out there will replace fiat currency. Governments rely on stability in their currency in order to manage their economies, and public blockchains are far too volatile and chaotic. More than likely, governments, like China has started to be, will leverage private blockchains to tokenize their fiat currencies into digital equivalents so that they can both take part, and compete, in the digital currency markets.

6. The Cryptocurrency Market Is Unregulated, and Fraud Is Common.

Governments around the world, at least those that have not outright banned Bitcoin and other altcoins, are still grappling with regulating the cryptocurrency market. Due to this, fraud is still common in the form of phishing, fraudulent ICOs, and even hacking. Crypto is also not insured, and while some exchanges and companies have some form of insurance, that is most often for their benefit and not yours. If you lose your coins, there is generally no easy way to get them back, if at all.

7. Go Into Investing With a Plan.

More than any other type of investment, crypto is not for the faint of heart. Do not just dive in headfirst and hope for the best. Make sure you have some form of plan and exit strategy in place before you buy your first coin or satoshi. More importantly, set a limit on how much you plan to invest. Remember, most financial experts will recommend investing no more than 10% of your portfolio directly in Bitcoin and other altcoins. Start small, and do not invest more than you can afford to lose.

8. Wallet Management is Key to Keeping Your Crypto Safe.Wallet Management Is Key to Keeping Your Crypto Safe.

While it is necessary to use a hot wallet when trading on an exchange, one should not keep all their coins in one basket. One does not have to look far to find stories of wallets being hacked and drained of their coins: We've already mentioned several such incidents. Ideally, any coins you are only holding and not actively using to trade or sell should be kept in a separate wallet, ideally, a cold wallet off the Internet.

9. Only Deal With Trusted Sources: Do Your Due Diligence.

When it comes to crypto, if something sounds too good to be true, it probably is or at least might have some caveat that could catch you by surprise. When dealing in crypto, only deal with reputable exchanges and other sources. If you are not sure, or even if you are sure, take the time to do some research. Again, don't jump in headfirst and hope for the best. This is particularly true for most ICOs and other start-ups, which are often a front for fraud.

10. Don't Stop Learning.

Everything we have presented to you in this book is just the proverbial tip of a very large cryptocurrency and crypto-investing iceberg. While this book strives to give you the best and most complete introduction into cryptocurrency and investing in the cryptocurrency market, it is just that: an introduction. There is still much more to learn, and new information comes out almost every day.

Thank you once again for taking the time to read this book. If you enjoyed it, please leave a review on Amazon. I read every review and they help new readers to discover my books.

Bonus:

Bitcoin Training Series

Bitcoin is an innovative payment network and a brand new kind of money. With this nine-part video course below, you'll find out all you need to know about buying and selling Bitcoin. This video course will show you the best way to obtain Bitcoins and the best investment strategies going forward.

Topics Covered: Section 1 (Bitcoin Investing)

- What Is Bitcoin?

- The Lowdown on Bitcoin Investing

- How Bitcoin Really Works

- How You Can Acquire Bitcoins

- Choosing the Right Bitcoin Wallet

- Getting Ready for Bitcoin Trading

- Real-Life Bitcoin Investment Strategies

- Avoid Bitcoin and Cryptocurrency Scams

- Bitcoin Investing: Best Practices

Topics Covered: Section 2 (Blockchain Technology)

- Three Important Things You Should Know About Cryptocurrency

- Four Key Areas for Developing Blockchain Platforms

- Four Things You Should Know Before Investing in Cryptocurrency

- Five Cryptocurrency Investment Tips That You Should Know

- Easy Tips for Getting Started in Cryptocurrency Trading

- How to Use Blockchain Technology

- The Top Things to Avoid With Cryptocurrency Investing

- Top Four Tips to Start Trading Cryptocurrencies

- Top Investment Tips for Trading in Cryptocurrency

- Understanding Three Different Types of Blockchain Technology

Topics Covered: Section 3 (Getting Paid In Bitcoin)

- How to Set Up a Rocketr

- How to Set Up a Bitcoin in Rocketr

- How to Add a Product

- How to Add a Pay Button

- Affiliate Marketing

- Coupons

- Email Marketing

- Blacklisting Buyers

Sign up for free today at https://bit.ly/3hm4cbI !

References

99 Bitcoins. (2021). *Bitcoin Obituaries.* 99Bitcoins. https://99bitcoins.com/bitcoin-obituaries/

101 Blockchains. (2021, May 31). *Top 10 Stablecoins of 2021.* 101 Blockchains. https://101blockchains.com/list-of-stablecoins/

Afreen, S. (2021, August 16). *Why is Blockchain Important and Why Does it Matters.* SimpliLearn. https://www.simplilearn.com/tutorials/blockchain-tutorial/why-is-blockchain-important

Agarwal, K. (2021, July 21). *Are There Taxes on Bitcoins?.* Investopedia. https://www.investopedia.com/articles/investing/040515/are-there-taxes-bitcoins.asp

Asic Miner Value (2021). *Miners Profitability.* ASIC Miner Value. https://www.asicminervalue.com/

Amplify ETFs. (2020). *Blok Amplify Transformational Data Sharing ETF.* Amplify ETFs. https://amplifyetfs.com/blok.html

Avan-Nomayo, O. (2021, July 15). *Bitcoin network node count sets new all-time high.* Cointelegraph. https://cointelegraph.com/news/bitcoin-network-node-count-sets-new-all-time-high

Bagtas, A. (2021, August 20). *Best Crypto Tax Software Pieces in 2021*. Review 42. https://review42.com/best/crypto-tax-software/

Barsby, O. (2021, August 27). *Diem Coin Release Date: When Will The Facebook Digital Coin Launch?*. Planet Crypto. https://www.gfinityesports.com/cryptocurrency/diem-coin-release-date-facebook-digital-coin-launch-libra-stablecoin-what-is-it/

Bavin, E. (2021, June 23). *$4.5bn lost: 5 biggest crypto scams of all time*. Yahoo! Finance. https://au.finance.yahoo.com/news/45-bn-lost-5-biggest-crypto-scams-of-all-time-215921732.html

Beigel, O. (2021, August 22). *Who Accepts Bitcoin as Payment?*. 99Bitcoins. https://99bitcoins.com/bitcoin/who-accepts/

Binance. (2021a). *Binance Staking, dedicated to increasing user staking income*. Binance. https://www.binance.com/en/defi-staking

Binance. (2021b). *Fiat Money vs. Cryptocurrency: Can They Co-Exist?*. Binance. https://www.binance.com/en/blog/421499824684902103/fiat/fiat-money-vs-cryptocurrency-can-they-coexist

Binance Academy. (2018, December 12). *Blockchain Advantages and Disadvantages*. Binance Academy. https://academy.binance.com/en/articles/positives-and-negatives-of-blockchain

Bitcoin Wikipedia. (2020, December 10). *Prokey*. Bitcoin Wiki. https://en.bitcoin.it/wiki/Prokey

Bizouati-Kennedy, Y. (2021, June 27). *Is Crypto Too Risky? 12 Experts Weigh In.* GoBankingRates. https://www.gobankingrates.com/investing/crypto/crypto-risky-12-experts-weigh-in/

BlockFi. (2021, February 4). *Top 5 Best Crypto Tax Software Companies.* BlockFI. https://blockfi.com/best-crypto-tax-software

Braddick, I. (2021, July 9). *HARD BARGAIN: Man who lost £275M fortune Bitcoin after tossing hard drive offers council £55Million to search landfill…but they say NO.* The Sun. https://www.thesun.co.uk/news/15541539/james-howells-275million-bitcoin-search-landfill-council-refuse/

Bram, B. (2021, August 23). *China's digital yuan is a warning to the world.* Wired. https://www.wired.co.uk/article/digital-yuan-china-bitcoin-libra

Browne, R. (2021, January 16). *Man makes last-ditch effort to recover $280 million in bitcoin he accidentally threw out.* CNBC. https://www.cnbc.com/2021/01/15/uk-man-makes-last-ditch-effort-to-recover-lost-bitcoin-hard-drive.html

Canellis, D. (2021). *Here's what a Bitcoin address does (and why you definitely shouldn't reuse it).* The Next Web. https://thenextweb.com/news/bitcoin-address-explained

Carter, S. M. (2017, December 20). Man accidentally threw away $127 million in bitcoin and officials won't allow a search. CNBC. https://www.cnbc.com/2017/12/20/man-lost-127-million-worth-of-bitcoins-and-city-wont-let-him-look.html

Coinbase. (2021) *Jump start your crypto portfolio.* Coinbase. https://www.coinbase.com/

Coin Ledger. (2021). *Crypto Taxes Done In Minutes.* CryptoTrader.Tax. https://cryptotrader.tax/

CoinMarketCap. (2021). *Today's Cryptocurrency Prices by Market Cap.* CoinMarketCap. https://coinmarketcap.com/

Cointelegraph. (2021). *How to mine Bitcoin: Everything you need to know.* Cointelegraph. *https://cointelegraph.com/bitcoin-for-beginners/how-to-mine-bitcoin-everything-you-need-to-know*

Cointelegraph. (2021). *ICO Vs IPO: Key Differences.* Cointelegraph. https://cointelegraph.com/ico-101/ico-vs-ipo-key-differences

Conway, C. (2021a, August 26). *Best Bitcoin Wallets.* Investopedia. https://www.investopedia.com/best-bitcoin-wallets-5070283

Conway, C. (2021b, June 28). *Best Crypto Exchanges.* Investopedia. https://www.investopedia.com/best-crypto-exchanges-5071855

Conway, C. (2021c, June 1). *Blockchain Explained.* Investopedia. https://www.investopedia.com/terms/b/blockchain.asp

Conway, C. (2021d, March 15). *Coinbase Review.* Investopedia. https://www.investopedia.com/tech/coinbase-what-it-and-how-do-you-use-it/

Conway, C. (2021e, June 21). *The 10 Most Important Cryptocurrencies Other Than Bitcoin.* Investopedia.

https://www.investopedia.com/tech/most-important-cryptocurrencies-other-than-bitcoin/

CryptoVantage. (2021). *ZenLedger Review*. CryptoVantage. https://www.cryptovantage.com/best-crypto-tax-software/zenledger/

CryptoVantage Staff. (2021a). *CryptoTrade.Tax Review*. CryptoVantage. https://www.cryptovantage.com/best-crypto-tax-software/cryptotrader-tax/

CryptoVantage Staff. (2021b). *TokenTax Review 2021*. CryptoVantage. https://www.cryptovantage.com/best-crypto-tax-software/tokentax/

Del Castillo, M, & Schifrin, M. (2020, February 19). *Blockchain 50*. Forbes. https://www.forbes.com/sites/michaeldelcastillo/2020/02/19/blockchain-50/?sh=5bf4618d7553

Deutsche Bank. (2021, July 14). *Digital Yuan: what is it and how does it work?*. Deutsche Bank. https://www.db.com/news/detail/20210714-digital-yuan-what-is-it-and-how-does-it-work?language_id=1

Diem Association. (2021). Welcome to the Diem project. Diem. https://www.diem.com/en-us/

Drake, N, Turner, B, & DeMuro, J. P. (2021, March 20). *Best cloud mining providers*. Techradar. https://www.techradar.com/best/cloud-mining-providers

Euromoney Learning. (2020). *The rise of private blockchains*. Euromoney.

https://www.euromoney.com/learning/blockchain-explained/the-rise-of-private-blockchains

Energyrates. (2021). *Crypto mining: Why Does Bitcoin Use so Much Energy?* energyrates.ca. https://energyrates.ca/crypto-mining-why-does-bitcoin-use-so-much-energy/

First Trust Portfolios L.P. (2021) *First Trust Indxx Innovative Transaction & Process ETF (LEGR).* First Trust. https://www.ftportfolios.com/retail/etf/etfsummary.aspx?Ticker=LEGR

Forkast. (2019, May 21). *What is Proof of Stake?.* Forkast. https://forkast.news/what-is-proof-of-stake/

Freeman Publications. (2021, February 20). *The Only Bitcoin Investing Book You'll Ever Need: An Absolute Beginner's Guide to the Cryptocurrency Which Is Changing the World and Your Finances in 2021 & Beyond.* Independently Published

Haar, R. (2019, August 12). *How Investors Can Get In On Crypto Without Actually Buying Any.* Next Advisor. https://time.com/nextadvisor/investing/cryptocurrency/how-to-invest-in-crypto-without-buying-any-crypto/

Farrington, R. (2021, May 17). *What Are The Risks Of Crypto Savings Accounts?* Forbes. https://www.forbes.com/sites/robertfarrington/2021/05/17/what-are-the-risks-of-crypto-savings-accounts/?sh=12a6acdf1417

Frankel, M. (2021, August 13). *7 Blockchain Stocks to Invest In.* The Motley Fool. https://www.fool.com/investing/stock-market/market-sectors/financials/blockchain-stocks/

Frankenfield, J. (2021a, April 12). *Tether (USDT)*. Investopedia. https://www.investopedia.com/terms/t/tether-usdt.asp

Frankenfield, J. (2021b, April 21). *Proof of Stake (PoS)*. Investopedia. https://www.investopedia.com/terms/p/proof-stake-pos.asp

Frankenfield, J. (2021c, August 17). *Binance Coin (BNB)*. Investopedia. https://www.investopedia.com/terms/b/binance-coin-bnb.asp

Frankenfield, J. (2021d, August 26). *51% Attack*. Investopedia. https://www.investopedia.com/terms/1/51-attack.asp

Frankenfield, J. (2021e, February 28). *Blockchain ETF*. Investopedia. https://www.investopedia.com/terms/b/blockchain-etf.asp

Frankenfield, J. (2021f, July 25). *Ethereum*. Investopedia. https://www.investopedia.com/terms/e/ethereum.asp

Frankenfield, J. (2021g, June 1). *What is Bitcoin?* Investopedia. https://www.investopedia.com/terms/b/bitcoin.asp

Frankenfield, J. (2021h, June 24). *Hard Fork (Blockchain)*. Investopedia. https://www.investopedia.com/terms/h/hard-fork.asp

Frankenfield, J. (2021i, March 26). *Mt. Gox*. Investopedia. https://www.investopedia.com/terms/m/mt-gox.asp

Frankenfield, J. (2021j, May 31). *Soft Fork*. Investopedia. https://www.investopedia.com/terms/s/soft-fork.asp

Graves, S, & Phillips D. (2021, July 16). *The 10 Public Companies With the Biggest Bitcoin Portfolios*. Decrypt. https://decrypt.co/47061/public-companies-biggest-bitcoin-portfolios

Handy, T. (2021, July 17). *10 Solutions You Need to Know for Your Cryptocurrency Exit Strategy*. thecapital. https://medium.com/the-capital/10-solutions-you-need-to-know-for-your-cryptocurrency-exit-strategy-a9f7c2c7357b

Hertig, A. (2020, December 30). *What is Proof-of-Stake?*. Coindesk. https://www.coindesk.com/proof-of-stake

Hong, E. (2021, May 4). *How does Bitcoin Mining Work?*. Investopedia. https://www.investopedia.com/tech/how-does-bitcoin-mining-work/

Horvath, S. (2021, August 18). *Best Crypto Savings Accounts For Earning Interest*. Benzinga. https://www.benzinga.com/money/crypto-savings-accounts/

Houston, R. (2021a, April 27). *Binance.US review: Crypto trading and staking rewards for US-based investors*. Business Insider. https://www.businessinsider.com/personal-finance/binanceus-investing-review

Houston, R. (2021b, July 28). *Coinbase Review: Crypto investing for individuals and institutions*. Business Insider. https://www.businessinsider.com/personal-finance/coinbase-investing-review

Houston, R. (2021c, August 4). *The best cryptocurrency exchanges for trading bitcoin and other assets.* Business Insider. https://www.businessinsider.com/personal-finance/best-crypto-bitcoin-exchanges

Jacquelyn. (2021, May 12). *Who Accepts Bitcoin and Ether Cryptocurrencies.* Currency Exchange International. https://www.ceifx.com/news/who-accepts-bitcoin-and-ether-cryptocurrencies

Juskalian, R. (2018, April 12). *Inside the Jordan refugee camp that runs on blockchain.* MIT Technology Review. https://www.technologyreview.com/2018/04/12/143410/inside-the-jordan-refugee-camp-that-runs-on-blockchain/

Kabir, U. (2021a). *5 Best Cryptocurrency Stocks to Invest in 2021.* Insider Monkey. https://www.insidermonkey.com/blog/5-best-cryptocurrency-stocks-to-invest-in-2021-951719/5/

Kabir, U. (2021b). *10 Biggest Companies and Hedge Funds Bullish on Ethereum.* Yahoo! Finance. https://finance.yahoo.com/news/10-biggest-companies-hedge-funds-140533907.html

Kabir, U. (2021c). *12 Best Cryptocurrency Stocks to invest in 2021.* Yahoo! Finance. https://finance.yahoo.com/news/12-best-cryptocurrency-stocks-invest-153023127.html

Karamat, S. (2018, May 21). *What is Hash Rate?.* Coin Rivet. https://coinrivet.com/guides/altcoins/what-is-hash-rate/

Kemmerer, D. (2021, August 26). *The Ultimate Crypto Tax Guide (2021).* CryptoTrader.Tax.

https://cryptotrader.tax/blog/the-traders-guide-to-cryptocurrency-taxes

Kent, P, & Bain, T. (2021). *What is Cryptocurrency Cloud Mining?* Dummies. https://www.dummies.com/personal-finance/investing/what-is-cloud-mining/

Kharpal, A. (2021, March 4). *China has given away millions in its digital yuan. This is how it works.* https://www.cnbc.com/2021/03/05/chinas-digital-yuan-what-is-it-and-how-does-it-work.html

Kimell, M. (2021, July 22). *Mt. Gox.* Coindesk. https://www.coindesk.com/company/mt-gox/

Kraken. (2021). *Earn Rewards by staking coins and fiat.* Kraken. https://www.kraken.com/features/staking-coins

La Place, J. (2021, December 14). *EY and Microsoft expand Xbox enterprise blockchain platform for rights and royalties management.* EY. https://www.ey.com/en_us/news/2020/12/ey-and-microsoft-expand-xbox-enterprise-blockchain-platform-for-rights-and-royalties-management

Ledger Academy. (2019, October 23). *Where are my coins?.* Ledger. https://www.ledger.com/academy/crypto/where-are-my-coins

Lioudis, N. (2021, April 27). *What is the Gold Standard?.* Investopedia. https://www.investopedia.com/ask/answers/09/gold-standard.asp

Lisa, A. (2021a, August 2). *Binance Coin (BNC): Why It's So Interesting to the Cryptocurrency World.* Yahoo! Finance. https://finance.yahoo.com/news/binance-coin-bnb-why-interesting-110049325.html

Lisa, A. (2021b, August 25). *10 Major Companies That Accept Bitcoin.* Yahoo! Finance. https://finance.yahoo.com/news/10-major-companies-accept-bitcoin-190340692.html

Lopatto, E. (2021, August 16). *The Tether Controversy, Explained.* Theverge. https://www.theverge.com/22620464/tether-backing-cryptocurrency-stablecoin

Mainfinex. (2021, August 21). *Could Cryptocurrency Replace Fiat Eventually? What Experts Say.* Medium. https://medium.com/@mainfinex/could-cryptocurrency-replace-fiat-eventually-what-experts-say-4efdd8a4ea97

Marshall, B. (2018, February 1). *How are transactions validated?.* Medium. https://medium.com/@blairlmarshall/how-do-miners-validate-transactions-c01b05f36231

Martindale J, & Forbes Vetted. (2021, July 19). The Best Crypto Wallets For Storing Bitcoin, Ethereum, Dogecoin And More. Forbes. https://www.forbes.com/sites/forbes-personal-shopper/2021/07/19/best-crypto-wallet/?sh=6ffb77b02b00

McNamara, R. (2021, August 18). *Best Cryptocurrency Wallets.* Benzinga. https://www.benzinga.com/money/best-crypto-wallet/#best-software-cryptocurrency-wallets

MEC Mining. (2020, November 4). *Top 5 Uses Of Gold – One Of The World's Most Coveted Metals.* MEC Mining. https://www.mecmining.com.au/top-5-uses-of-gold-one-of-the-worlds-most-coveted-metals/

Mehta, N, Agashe, A, & Detroja, P. (2019, June 12). *Blockchain Bubble or Revolution: The Future of Bitcoin, Blockchains, and Cryptocurrencies.* Paravane Ventures

Mitra, R. (2021, June 4). *5 Best Hardware Wallets: [The Most Comprehensive List] – Blockgeeks.* Blockgeeks. https://blockgeeks.com/guides/best-hardware-wallets-comparative-list-blockgeeks/

Nadeau, M. (2021, May 6). *Cryptojacking explained: How to prevent, detect, and recover from it.* Csoonline. https://www.csoonline.com/article/3253572/what-is-cryptojacking-how-to-prevent-detect-and-recover-from-it.html

Newberry, E. (2021, August 3). *3 Reasons to Be Cautious About Tether.* The Ascent. https://www.fool.com/the-ascent/cryptocurrency/articles/3-reasons-to-be-cautious-about-tether/

Noone, G. (2021, May 17). *The case against bitcoin: Why governments are cracking down on crypto.* Tech Monitor. https://techmonitor.ai/policy/digital-economy/case-against-bitcoin-governments-plan-cryptocurrency-ban

NVIDIA Corporation. (2021). *NVIDIA CMP HX.* NVIDIA. https://www.nvidia.com/en-us/cmp/

Paypal. (2021). *Crypto for the people.* Paypal. https://www.paypal.com/us/webapps/mpp/crypto

Pollock, D. (2020, February 27). *Blockchain For Good: How The United Nations is Looking To Leverage Technology.* Forbes. https://www.forbes.com/sites/darrynpollock/2020/02/27/blockchain-for-good-how-the-united-nations-is-looking-to-leverage-technology/?sh=28bccd11543d

Reiff, N. (2021a). *3 Blockchain ETFs for Q4 2021.* Investopedia. https://www.investopedia.com/news/3-blockchain-etfs-buy-2018/

Reiff, N. (2021b). *How to Identify Cryptocurrency and ICO Scams.* Investopedia. https://www.investopedia.com/tech/how-identify-cryptocurrency-and-ico-scams/

Reiff, N. (2021c). *Were There Cryptocurrencies Before Bitcoin?.* Investopedia. https://www.investopedia.com/tech/were-there-cryptocurrencies-bitcoin/

Robertson, J. (2021, August 11). *Best Crypto ETFs.* Benzinga. https://www.benzinga.com/money/best-crypto-etfs/

Seth, S. (2021, August 25). *How Do Cryptocurrency Mining Pools Work?.* Investopedia. https://www.investopedia.com/tech/how-do-mining-pools-work/

Sharma, T.K. (2020a). *Public vs. Private Blockchain: A Comprehensive Comparison.* Blockchain Council. https://www.blockchain-council.org/blockchain/public-vs-private-blockchain-a-comprehensive-comparison/

Sharma, T.K. (2020b). *Top 10 Companies That Have Already Adopted Blockchain.* Blockchain Council.

https://www.blockchain-council.org/blockchain/top-10-companies-that-have-already-adopted-blockchain/

Sherter, A. (2021, June 22). *Bitcoin crash wipes out nearly all the cryptocurrency's gains for 2021*. CBS News. https://www.cbsnews.com/news/bitcoin-price-2021-gains/

Sigalos, M. (2021, May 5). *You don't actually own the bitcoin you buy on PayPal. But you can still make a profit*. CNBC. https://www.cnbc.com/2021/05/05/investing-in-bitcoin-with-paypal-what-you-should-know.html

Singhai, R, & ET Contributors. (2021, August 8). *Gold vs Bitcoin: Which one is a better option for investment?*. Economictimes.indiatimes. https://economictimes.indiatimes.com/markets/crypto currency/gold-vs-bitcoin-which-one-is-a-better-option-for-investment/articleshow/85148997.cms?from=mdr

SirenETFs. (2020). *Siren Nasdaq NexGen Economy ETF (BLCN)*. SirenETFs. https://www.sirenetfs.com/siren-nasdaq-nexgen-economy-etf-blcn/

Sobers, R. (2021, January 29). *What Is Cryptojacking? Prevention and Detection Tips*. Varonis. https://www.varonis.com/blog/cryptojacking/

Spadafora, A. (2021, August 24) *Coinbase customers up in arms after hackers drain crypto wallets*. Techradar. https://www.techradar.com/news/coinbase-customers-up-in-arms-after-hackers-drain-crypto-wallets

Statt, N. (2020, March 3). *Facebook is shifting its Libra cryptocurrency plans after intense regulatory pressure*. The Verge.

https://www.theverge.com/2020/3/3/21163658/face book-libra-cryptocurrency-token-ditching-plans-calibra-wallet-delay

Stempel, J. (2021, September 1). *U.S. SEC charges BitConnect founder with $2 bln cryptocurrency fraud.* Reuters. https://www.reuters.com/technology/us-sec-sues-bitconnect-founder-over-alleged-2-bln-cryptocurrency-fraud-2021-09-01/

Tattersall, S. (2019). *Public Addresses & Private Keys.* Beginner's Guide to Cryptocurrencies. http://www.beginnersguidetocryptocurrencies.com/keys.html

Tepper, T, & Schmidt, J. (2021, August 1). *Best Crypto Exchanges of 2021.* Forbes Advisor. https://www.forbes.com/advisor/investing/best-crypto-exchanges/

TokenTax. (2021). *Calculate your crypto taxes and file your return.* TokenTax. https://tokentax.co/

Vasic, L. (2021a, June 9). *San Jose Sharks to Accept Crypto in First for NHL Team.* SportTechie. https://www.sporttechie.com/san-jose-sharks-to-accept-crypto-in-first-for-nhl-team#:~:text=MLB's%20Oakland%20Athletics%2C%20the%20NHL's,cryptocurrency%20from%20fans%20buying%20tickets.

Vasic, L. (2021b, March 5). *Dallas Mavericks Accepting Dogecoin for Tickets, Merchandise.* SportTechie. https://www.sporttechie.com/dallas-mavericks-accepting-dogecoin-for-tickets-merchandise?utm_source=SportTechie_Newsletter&ut

m_medium=Email&utm_campaign=SPRTCD2106030
02&oly_enc_id=

Vega, N. (2021, February 18). *Bitcoin passed %50,000 – here's what you need to about the popular cryptocurrency.* CNBC Make It. https://www.cnbc.com/2021/02/18/bitcoin-passed-50000-dollars-heres-what-you-need-to-know.html

Verrender, I. (2021, May 2). *Will Bitcoin replace gold as the ultimate store of wealth?.* ABC News. https://www.abc.net.au/news/2021-05-03/the-great-bitcoin-challenge-can-it-topple-gold-/100111226

Walsh, D. (2021, August 30). *Paying with Bitcoin: These are the major companies that accept crypto as payment.* Euronews.next. https://www.euronews.com/next/2021/08/29/paying-with-cryptocurrencies-these-are-the-major-companies-that-accept-cryptos-as-payment

Wielen, Z.V.D. (2021, April 30). *Crypto exit strategy – When to sell your coins.* Anycoindirect.eu. https://anycoindirect.eu/en/blog/crypto-exit-strategy-when-to-sell-your-coins

Wikipedia Foundation. (2021a). *Application-specific integrated circuit.* Wikipedia. https://en.wikipedia.org/wiki/Application-specific_integrated_circuit

Wikipedia Foundation. (2021b). *Bitcoin Cash.* Wikipedia. https://en.wikipedia.org/wiki/Bitcoin_Cash

Wikipedia Foundation. (2021c). *Bitcoin.* Wikipedia. https://en.wikipedia.org/wiki/Bitcoin

Wikipedia Foundation. (2021d). *Bitconnect.* Wikipedia. https://en.wikipedia.org/wiki/Bitconnect

Wikipedia Foundation. (2021e). *Blockchain.* Wikipedia. https://en.wikipedia.org/wiki/Blockchain

Wikipedia Foundation. (2021f). *Cardano (blockchain platform).* Wikipedia. https://en.wikipedia.org/wiki/Cardano_(blockchain_pl atform)

Wikipedia Foundation. (2021g). *Cryptocurrency Wallet.* Wikipedia. https://en.wikipedia.org/wiki/Cryptocurrency_wallet

Wikipedia Foundation. (2021h). *Cryptocurrency.* Wikipedia. https://en.wikipedia.org/wiki/Cryptocurrency

Wikipedia Foundation. (2021i). *Decentralized application.* Wikipedia. https://en.wikipedia.org/wiki/Decentralized_applicatio n

Wikipedia Foundation. (2021j). *Decentralized finance.* Wikipedia. Wikipedia. https://en.wikipedia.org/wiki/Decentralized_finance

Wikipedia Foundation. (2021k). *Diem (digital currency).* Wikipedia. https://en.wikipedia.org/wiki/Diem_(digital_currency)

Wikipedia Foundation. (2021l). *Digicash.* https://en.wikipedia.org/wiki/DigiCash

Wikipedia Foundation. (2021m). *Digital Renminbi.* Wikipedia. https://en.wikipedia.org/wiki/Digital_renminbi

Wikipedia Foundation. (2021n). *Dogecoin*. Wikipedia. https://en.wikipedia.org/wiki/Dogecoin

Wikipedia Foundation. (2021o). *Economics of bitcoin*. Wikipedia. https://en.wikipedia.org/wiki/Economics_of_bitcoin

Wikipedia Foundation. (2021p). *Ethereum*. Wikipedia. https://en.wikipedia.org/wiki/Ethereum

Wikipedia Foundation. (2021q). *Fork (blockchain)*. Wikipedia. https://en.wikipedia.org/wiki/Fork_(blockchain

Wikipedia Foundation. (2021r). *Hashcash*. Wikipedia. https://en.wikipedia.org/wiki/Hashcash

Wikipedia Foundation. (2021s). *Initial coin offering*. Wikipedia. https://en.wikipedia.org/wiki/Initial_coin_offering

Wikipedia Foundation. (2021t). *Mt. Gox*. Wikipedia. https://en.wikipedia.org/wiki/Mt._Gox

Wikipedia Foundation. (2021u). *Satoshi (unit)*. Wikipedia. https://en.bitcoin.it/wiki/Satoshi_(unit)

Wikipedia Foundation. (2021v). *Satoshi Nakamoto*. Wikipedia. https://en.wikipedia.org/wiki/Satoshi_Nakamoto

Wikipedia Foundation. (2021w). *Security token offering*. Wikipedia. https://en.wikipedia.org/wiki/Security_token_offering

Wikipedia Foundation. (2021x). *Silk Road (Marketplace)*. Wikipedia. https://en.wikipedia.org/wiki/Silk_Road_(marketplace)

Wikipedia Foundation. (2021y). *SIM swap scam*. Wikipedia. https://en.wikipedia.org/wiki/SIM_swap_scam

Wikipedia Foundation. (2021z). *Smart Contract*. Wikipedia. https://en.wikipedia.org/wiki/Smart_contract

Wikipedia. (2021a). *Stablecoin*. Wikipedia. https://en.wikipedia.org/wiki/Stablecoin

Wikipedia. (2021b). *Tether (cryptocurrency)*. Wikipedia. https://en.wikipedia.org/wiki/Tether_(cryptocurrency)

Wikipedia. (2021c). *WeChat*. Wikipedia. https://en.wikipedia.org/wiki/WeChat

YCharts. (2021). *Bitcoin Average Confirmation Time*. YCharts. https://ycharts.com/indicators/bitcoin_average_confir mation_time

Zamost, S, Javers, E, Schlesinger, J, Council, S, & Serran-Román, A. (2021, August 24). *Coinbase slammed for what users say is terrible customer service after hackers drain their accounts*. CNBC. https://www.cnbc.com/2021/08/24/coinbase-slammed-for-terrible-customer-service-after-hackers-drain-user-accounts.html

ZenLedger. (2021). *Simpli DeFi and Crypt Taxes for Investors and Tax Professionals*. ZenLedger. https://www.zenledger.io/

www.ingramcontent.com/pod-product-compliance
Lightning Source LLC
Chambersburg PA
CBHW011843200326
41597CB00026B/4682